NERY, 1914

THE ADVENTURE

OF THE

GERMAN 4TH CAVALRY DIVISION

ON THE

31ST AUGUST AND THE 1ST SEPTEMBER

MAJOR A. F. BECKE
(LATE R.F.A.)

The Naval & Military Press Ltd

published in association with

FIREPOWER
The Royal Artillery Museum
Woolwich

Published by
The Naval & Military Press Ltd
Unit 10 Ridgewood Industrial Park,
Uckfield, East Sussex,
TN22 5QE England
Tel: +44 (0) 1825 749494
Fax: +44 (0) 1825 765701
www.naval-military-press.com

in association with

FIREPOWER
The Royal Artillery Museum, Woolwich
www.firepower.org.uk

In reprinting in facsimile from the original, any imperfections are inevitably reproduced and the quality may fall short of modern type and cartographic standards.

NERY.   The Square in front of the Church.

NERY.   Farm held by B. Squadron, 11th Hussars,

NERY, 1914.

The adventure of the German *4th Cavalry Division* on the 31st August and the 1st September.[1]

By Major A. F. Becke, late R.F.A.

(With 5 sketches and 4 photographs.)

" . . . . From black defeat and crimsoned dust,
See golden victory rise ! "

Whyte Melville.

PART I. THE PURSUIT.

THE OPENING OF THE CAMPAIGN.   THE INVASION OF BELGIUM.

Sketch 1.

AT the opening of the war, the *4th Cavalry Division*, forming part of *Marwitz's II Cavalry Corps (H.K.K.II.)*, advanced through Belgium to clear the way for the advance of the *First* and *Second Armies* towards the line Antwerp—Brussels—Charleroi.[2] In this advance there were several sharp fights with the slowly retiring Belgian Army. Among these engagements perhaps the most notable was the fight at Haelen on the 12th August, in which the *4th Cavalry Division* was hotly engaged, four of its regiments

---

[1] This story of the German Operations is based on Kluck's *March on Paris*, Poseck's *German Cavalry in Belgium and France*, the German Official Account, and such Regimental Histories as are available. My most grateful thanks are due to Miss Blackwood for the translations of the accounts of the *18th Dragoons* and of the *15th Hussars*. The British positions are taken from Vol. I of our Official History (2nd Edition), and the French dispositions are those given on the maps with Part 2 of Vol. I of their Official History. The account of *The Fight at Nery*, by the author, published in the R.U.S.I. Journal, May, 1919, has also been used for British dispositions, and readers are referred to it for a more detailed account of the British operations at Nery. General T. T. Pitman's article on *The Attack on the 1st Cavalry Brigade at Nery* (*Cavalry Journal, April, 1920*) has also been used. My most grateful thanks are also due to Major-General T. T. Pitman, C.B., C.M.G., for much additional information and assistance, and for the loan of some very interesting photographs of the village and of the battlefield. I am also deeply indebted to Captain C. Falls for reading through the manuscript and making many valuable suggestions.

Further information from officers who were present at the action has also been received, since the publication of *Nery*, and it has been incorporated in this narrative.

To assist the reader the names of all German units are printed in italics throughout the text and on the sketches. Greenwich times are employed; and all accents have been omitted except those occurring on penultimate or final e's.

[2] For a general Order of Battle of that part of the German *Right Wing* that was involved see Appendix I, and for a detailed order of battle of the *4th Cavalry Division* see Appendix II.

being badly mauled.[1] As well as taking part in the fight the division on this day covered no less than thirty miles.

On the day of Mons, the 23rd August, Marwitz's Cavalry was halted on the Schelde, thirty miles away to the north-westward, guarding against an imaginary British advance from Ostend, Dunkirk, and Calais. The fog of war having been dissipated by the fighting at Mons, *H.K.K.II.* on the 24th marched rapidly southwards to overtake the *First Army* now engaged in the pursuit of the B.E.F. The advance of the *First* and *Second Armies* through Belgium was completed, the country had been overrun, and only one of its fortresses, Antwerp, was left unviolated in the long ruin-strewn path of the conquerors.[2]

THE INVASION OF FRANCE.

Early on the 26th *H.K.K.II.* struck into the centre and left wing of General Smith Dorrien's force which was holding the le Cateau position. As the *4th Cavalry Division*, in the centre near Bethencourt, was soon reinforced by the infantry of the right wing of the *8th Division (IV Corps)*, it never became so heavily engaged as its sister divisions, the *2nd* and *9th*, and thus its losses were comparatively light. After le Cateau the B.E.F. withdrew in a southerly direction, but the *First Army* and *H.K.K.II.* swung away south-westwards. As the *Second Army* continued to follow Lanrezac's Army, a widening gap was created between Kluck and Bülow, and this gap happened to cover the front on which the B.E.F. was retiring.

On the 28th Kluck's advance collided with the leading troops of the French Sixth Army, and the feeble resistance offered to the German onrush, coupled with the sudden disappearance of the B.E.F., tended to make Kluck believe that final victory was in sight and that he could race on, taking almost any risk. "The pace of the pursuit became almost that of a hunt."

---

[1] The losses suffered at Haelen were as follows:—

		Officers	men	horses
	2nd *Cuirassier Regt.*	6	71	270
	9th *Uhlans*	4	100	250
	17th *Dragoons*	8	159	165
and	18th *Dragoons*	6	138	163

The *15th* and *16th Hussars* do not appear to have been seriously engaged on the 12th.

[2] The Belgian Army, of six divisions and a cavalry division, retired to Antwerp which was then masked by the *III Reserve Corps*.

It must be remembered that Liege had fulfilled its appointed task as a *fort d'arrêt*; and that Namur, despite its obsolete defences and guns, had justified itself.

NERY, 1914.

SKETCH I

The Advance of the 4th Cavalry Division through Belgium & Northern France in August, 1914.

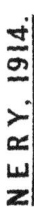

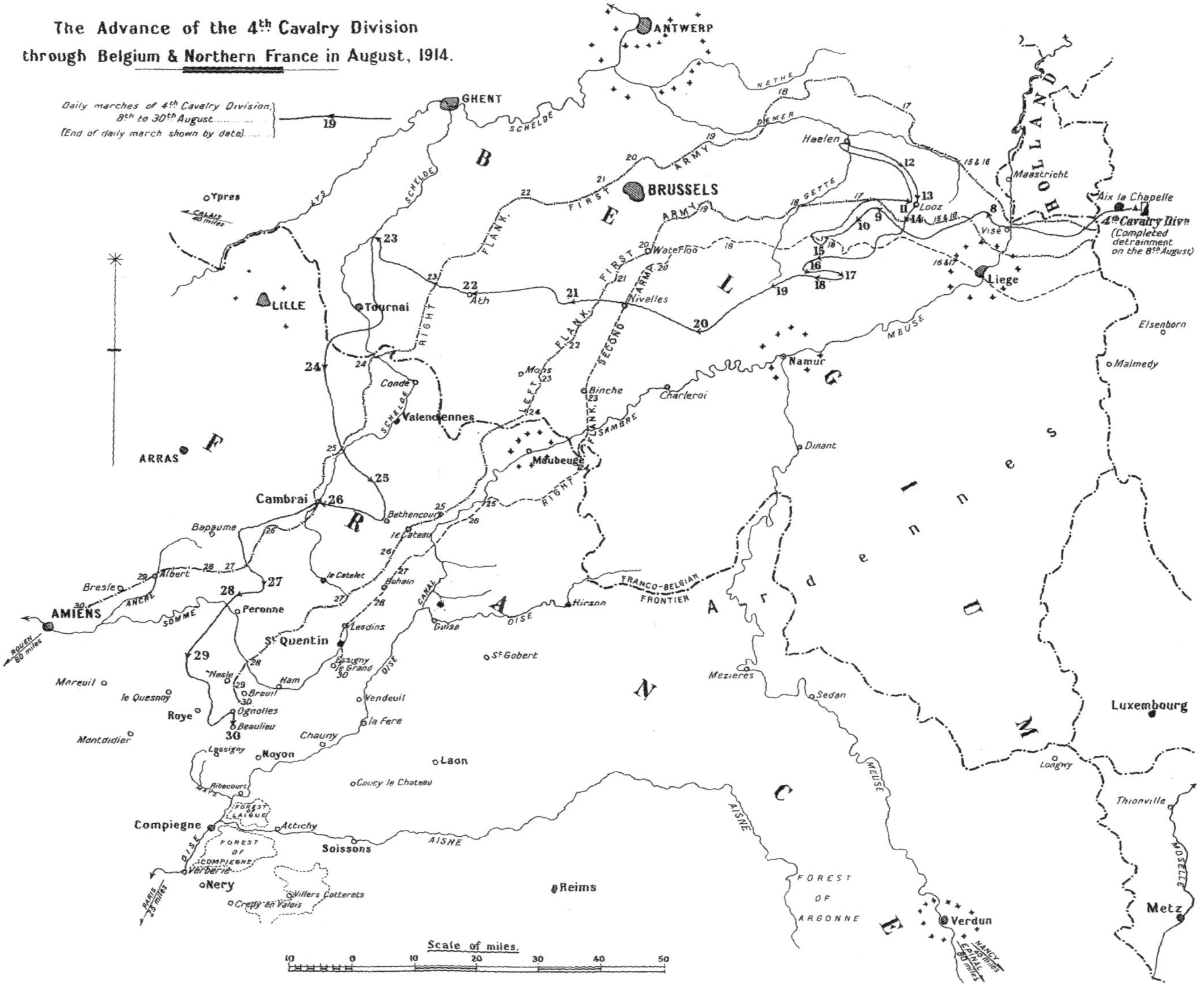

NERY, 1914.

The eastward swing of the German right wing.

On the 30th, to ensure that full advantage was obtained from the supposed victory just gained at Guise by the *Second Army* over Lanrezac, Kluck decided to open an energetic pursuit heading in a south-easterly direction for the line Noyon—Compiegne, and *Supreme Command* approved this alteration. It was at this moment, as Stegemann declares, that the German operations had reached "the highest point of strategic success." But within ten days occurred a dramatic change in the course of the war.

Situation of the *First Army* and of H.K.K.II. and H.K.K.I. on the 30th.

Sketch 1.

By the evening of this day the corps of the *First Army* had reached the following line:—the *IV Reserve* halted about 8 miles north-east of Amiens, the *II* about Moreuil, the *IV* about le Quesnoy, the *III* around Roye; and the *18th Division (IX Corps)* to the east of Roye; whilst the *17th Division (IX)*, which had been co-operating with Bülow during the Battle of Guise, halted to the south of St. Quentin. The *Second Army* on this day occupied a line astride the Oise stretching from Essigny le Grand through St. Gobert.

The responsibility of protecting Kluck's left flank on the 30th fell on *Marwitz's Cavalry Corps*. Hostile troops had been reported to be at Noyon and *H.K.K.II.* pushed on to cover Kluck's advance from this direction, but no serious action with the retiring enemy took place, and the three cavalry divisions, with the *4th* leading, halted for the night to the north-west of Noyon.

Richthofen's I. Cavalry Corps (H.K.K.I.), co-operating with Bülow, was faced with the Oise valley. The proximity of la Fere and the breadth of the valley near Chauny caused Richthofen to consider that a crossing was inadvisable in this neighbourhood. He decided, therefore, to capture Noyon, break through there, and then operate against the French left. But when *H.K.K.I.* reached Noyon the town had already been evacuated and most of the Oise bridges had been blown up. The river here is a considerable obstacle, being about 80 yards wide and some 9 to 10 feet in depth. In this section it is also accompanied by the Sambre—

Oise canal, itself about 25 yards broad. It was ascertained that so far the bridge at Ribecourt was intact and it was most important for any further advance. A well-handled patrol from the *Guard Cavalry Division* seized the bridge and prevented its demolition, and a cyclist detachment from the division was then sent forward to secure it. The two divisions then halted for the night on the right bank of the river. The gap separating the inner flanks of *H.K.K.II.* and *H.K.K.I.* was only about six miles.

The distance marched so far had been considerable. The main body of the *4th Cavalry Division* had covered at least four hundred miles in the twenty-three days that had elapsed since its detrainment at Aix-la-Chapelle. Nor does this take into consideration the long distances necessarily traversed in reconnaissance duties, by despatch riders and by patrols, and the various movements that had been made during the numerous actions that had been fought. This advance too had been carried out in an exceptionally warm August and without a single rest day. Heavy as had been the demands already made upon it, the division, no longer fresh or at full strength, was about to be much more severely tested.

THE B.E.F. ON THE 30TH AND 31ST.

Sketch 2.

The Battle of Guise, the fighting on the Somme, and Kluck's south-westerly advance, had so relieved the direct pressure on the B.E.F. that Sir John French ordered his army to halt and rest on the 29th, provided all the formations were south of the line Vendeuil—Ham—Nesle.[1] The retirement was resumed on the 30th and a great effort was made to place the Aisne, a stream about fifty yards wide and some six feet in depth, between the British and their pursuers. By nightfall, however, only the 2nd Cavalry Brigade, the II Corps, the 4th Division, and the 19th Infantry Brigade,[2] had crossed the river.

G.H.Q. Operation Order No. 12, issued at 6.15 p.m. on the 30th, directed that on the 31st the Cavalry should protect the left flank, moving down the right (or western) bank of the Oise. The order then allotted the following night billeting areas to the

---

[1] G.H.Q. Operation Order No. 10 of the 28th.

[2] The III Corps, consisting of the 4th Division and the 19th Infantry Brigade, was only formed on the 31st. A corps operation order was issued that night.

various formations:—to the Cavalry Division, the area Rivecourt—Bazicourt—Sarron (on the right bank of the Oise); to the 4th Division and the 19th Infantry Brigade [i.e. the III Corps], the area Verberie—Pontpoint—Saintines——St. Sauveur; and to the II Corps, the area Morienval—Bethisy—Nery—Crepy—Feigneux—Fresnoy. Thus the order placed certain areas at the disposal of formations for passing the night, all or part of which they might occupy as convenient. It did not fix the front to be held, or the boundaries between which formations would be responsible for protection. Such instructions were likely to lead to misconceptions, and "to the rather amateur wording of this particular order much of what happened on the 1st September can be directly traced."

On the 31st the I Corps crossed the Aisne, whilst the II Corps pushed on to Crepy en Valois, and the III Corps halted at and near Verberie. The 1st Cavalry Brigade and "L" Battery, R.H.A., with whose fortunes on the 1st September we shall be particularly concerned, reconnoitred widely on the right bank of the Oise and found no trace of an enemy.[1]

Actually the cavalry found that most of its billeting area was already occupied by the French Provisional Cavalry Division (formed from Sordet's Cavalry Corps) that was operating with Maunoury's Sixth Army, and only the 2nd Cavalry Brigade could be accommodated on the right bank of the river. The 4th Cavalry Brigade and divisional headquarters billeted close to Verberie in the 4th Divisional area, and Brig.-Genl. C. J. Briggs, C.B., commanding the 1st Cavalry Brigade, was informed that the village of Nery, belonging to the II Corps, was not occupied and that it could be used by his brigade. But General Briggs was not informed that the II Corps was not using any of the villages in its area west of Crepy or that the outposts of the II Corps and of the 4th Division (with the 19th Brigade) did not more than cover their own billets and did not join up. Thus Nery lay in a large gap between the above formations and was not covered, as General Briggs naturally assumed it was, by a general outpost line.

After recrossing the Oise at Verberie, the 1st Cavalry Brigade

---

[1] As we shall see later on and as is clear from Sketch 2, *H.K.K.II.* moved east when the 1st Cavalry Brigade was moving west, and *H.K.K.II.* being some miles to the northward in the Matz valley the two cavalries never even sighted one another that morning.

passed through the small town just as the 4th Division was reaching it after an exhausting march through the Forest of Compiegne. The three cavalry regiments then moved on to Nery, and reaching the village about 6 p.m. the officers and men received a warm welcome from the inhabitants.

Under the special circumstances existing during the retreat the standing arrangements in the 1st Cavalry Brigade for protection at night were broadly as follows:—Each unit was responsible for the defence and security of that portion of a village that was allotted to it, and for patrolling the roads leading into its sector. In the event of a night attack each unit would hold its own sector and fight on its own ground. On arrival at Nery, the 5th Dragoon Guards were allotted the north end of the village, the 11th Hussars billeted in the middle, and the Queen's Bays were placed on the west side of the main street with a squadron bivouacking in a field to the south-west. Brigade Headquarters were established in a house on the east side of the main street.

As it was growing dark when the Brigade was assembled at Nery, the issue of detailed outpost orders was out of the question, and as it was considered that the bivouacs were already covered by a general outpost line the usual protective arrangements were made and each unit was instructed to guard its own perimeter. The 11th Hussars, the regiment responsible for the centre of the village, reconnoitred the ridge to the east. Two alternative arrangements were possible: either the ridge must be held by a complete unit, or else the edge of the village must be held and the ridge patrolled. The eastern ridge did not offer any specially favourable position for defence, and it would be difficult either to support or to withdraw the unit holding it. Further it must also be remembered that when Nery was reached in the retreat, the men had had no proper sleep for ten days and another very early start had been ordered for the next day. It was therefore decided, unfortunately as events proved, to hold the edge of the village only and to patrol the ridge early in the morning.

"L" Battery (Major the Hon. W. D. Sclater-Booth), meanwhile, had halted in Verberie so as to water there and thus lessen the difficulty of watering so many horses late in the day at a small village. Thus "L" only reached Nery about dusk, and found that the sugar-factory and a field on the south side of the village had been assigned to it. The Brigade now began to settle down into its quarters for the night, knowing that the retreat was to be continued at 4.30 a.m. on the morrow.[1] The 5th Dragoon Guards covered the northern end of the village, the Bays were responsible for the south, whilst "L" battery was directed to block the two roads that led east and south from the vicinity of the sugar factory. Except for the piquets, horses and men slept and silence soon brooded over the village.

A glance at Sketch 2 will show that the position of the 1st Cavalry Brigade was far from enviable, though it appeared to be secure enough, for no enemy had been sighted on the right bank of the Oise. But it was not on the north-west side that the real menace lurked. Away to the north in the great forest tract that lay between Aisne and Oise danger was gathering, and the approaches from the forest to Nery lay open.

Actually on the 31st the British had gleaned very little information about the German movements. One hostile cavalry division, however, had been seen by an air observer as it moved eastwards outside the northern edge of the Forest of Laigue.[2] But of the advance of the *4th Cavalry Division* no sign was discernible. This no doubt was due to the fact that Garnier moved down the Matz valley, crossed the Oise fairly early, and then plunged into the leafy glades of the Forest of Laigue. Halting then as he did until 5 p.m. in the forest, the Division was unlikely to be noticed from the air. Further one observer, who flew at an altitude of between 4000 and 5000 feet above the forest, reported that "the woods were minutely examined and no enemy was observed, but the conditions were unfavourable for observation over woods owing to a haze."

Thus nothing really occurred during the daylight hours to threaten the further unmolested retreat of the B.E.F. With its western flank now in touch across the Oise with the flank of Maunoury's Army, and the pressure taken off the eastern flank by Lanrezac's resolute stand at Guise, it appeared likely that the retirement on the 1st September might be as uneventful as that which had just been performed.

---

[1] Summer time had not been introduced, and sunrise was about 5.15 a.m.
[2] It belonged to *H.K.K.I.*

It is now time to see what the Germans were doing on the 31st, and what were their plans and hopes for the 1st September.

THE GERMAN RIGHT WING ON THE 31ST AUGUST.

Kluck, true to the maxim that in war "Sweat saves blood!" ordered his troops to carry out another long march on the 31st. He had determined to neglect Maunoury and the B.E.F., and to wheel round definitely towards the Oise, moving through Noyon and Compiegne, and to exploit the success gained by the *Second Army*. *Supreme Command* gave its approval to this plan. By nightfall the *First Army* was placed in two large groups in echelon, the right group being in rear between Montdidier and the Oise, whilst the left group had reached the lower Aisne. The Corps halted as follows:—the *IV Reserve Corps* was at Ailly, covering the right rear, the right group, consisting of the *II* and *IV Corps*, was between Maignelay and Mareuil; in the left group, the *III Corps* had reached the north bank of the Aisne at Attichy and Vic, but the divisions of the *IX Corps* were still separated, the *18th* halting to the north-westward of Soissons, whilst the *17th* had only reached St. Simon. *First Army Headquarters* moved forward from Peronne to Noyon. Placed as the *First Army* was, it had become a distinct menace to the B.E.F.; but the stroke with which Kluck hoped to complete Lanrezac's destruction was not delivered on the 1st as a deadly thrust at the Fifth Army, but fell merely as a succession of blows on the corps of the B.E.F.

The *Second Army* halted for the day, resting and reorganising on the line reached on the 30th. The punishment meted out by Lanrezac had been so severe that he was just able to slip clear of his pursuers.

THE GERMAN CAVALRY ON THE 31ST AUGUST.

H.K.K.I.

Richthofen's principal task was to delay the retirement of Lanrezac's Army for a sufficient time to allow Bülow to overhaul it, and to give Kluck a chance to strike into its flank and rear. To achieve this end *H.K.K.I.* was ordered to cross the Oise by the suspension bridge at Ribecourt and push eastward in the direction of Soissons, so as to reach a position which would enable the cavalry to delay the French from leaving la Fere and Laon. Despite a couple of brushes with the enemy on the 31st, by evening *H.K.K.I.* had got behind Lanrezac (as shown on Sketch 2) but did not venture to attack, as the enemy was in overwhelming strength and no infantry support could be expected within a reasonable time.

H.K.K.II.

Marwitz's Cavalry was also intended to move against the left flank of Lanrezac's Army, and on the evening of the 30th Kluck ordered *H.K.K.II.* to cross the Oise on the 31st, moving above Compiegne, and, ignoring the B.E.F. and Maunoury's Army, to push forward in the direction of Soissons. When the advance began on the 31st the five *Jäger* battalions were to cover the exposed right flank of the cavalry from any attack from the direction of Montdidier. Once the Oise had been crossed this danger would naturally disappear, and then the *Jäger* were to press on by a forced march towards Crepy en Valois, which they were to reach on the 1st September.[1] The *4th Cavalry Division* led the advance of Marwitz's Cavalry, but it will be better to glance briefly at the movements of the *2nd* and *9th Cavalry Divisions* before giving in detail the work of the *4th* on this day.

The *2nd* crossed the Oise above Thourotte and advancing through the Forest of Laigue proceeded to reconnoitre beyond its eastern edge. Meanwhile General von der Marwitz, who was at that time with the *4th Cavalry Division* at Offemont, heard of the presence of strong hostile columns near Soissons, Vic, Villers Cotterets, and Crepy, and so at 4 p.m. he ordered that a vigorous pursuit should be carried out through the night in the direction of Nanteuil le Haudouin. Thus the direction of Marwitz's advance was completely altered and his divisions now turned south. Crossing the Aisne the three divisions were to concentrate at Rozieres on the morrow, and thus drive a deep wedge into the Allied front. Actually only one sorely harassed and battered division, no longer a serious fighting force, reached its destination on the 1st September.

The *9th Cavalry Division* also crossed the Oise and by 5 p.m. it had reached Choisy where it received the new orders. So as to carry out General von der Marwitz's instructions the *2nd Division* moved

---

[1] Here on the 1st the *Jäger* became engaged with the 5th Division which had halted overnight at Crepy.

back to Choisy, halting there from 7 until 9 p.m. The General himself had decided to move with this division, which then followed the *9th* southward through Compiegne and the Forest of Compiegne past la Croix St. Ouen towards Verberie. Soon after reaching St. Ouen the *9th Cavalry Division* came under fire, undoubtedly from the outposts of the 4th Division blocking the road in front of Verberie.

Marwitz received a report of what had happened and promptly ordered the *9th* to attack Verberie and force a way through. But the *9th* was completely exhausted and action in the darkness in the forest against an enemy of unknown strength, whose position could not be defined, was practically impossible, and the worn-out division finally bivouacked on the main road and awaited the dawn before delivering any further attack. The *2nd Cavalry Division* closed up on the *9th* and then halted alongside it for the rest of the night.

At 10 p.m. a wireless message from *First Army* was taken in. This stated that the Army would cross the line Compiegne—Ambleny at 7 a.m. on the 1st, and would push on to Verberie, Villers Cotterets, and Longpont before halting for the night. *H.K.K.II* was ordered to attack the enemy left wing retiring from Soissons past Villers Cotterets. But General von Kluck did not yet know of Marwitz's afternoon swing to the southward. General Marwitz, too, was quite out of touch with his *4th Division* which was swallowed up somewhere in the forest to the east.

It is now time to narrate the advance of the *4th Cavalry Division* on the 31st.

4th Cavalry Division, 31st August.

Overnight the Division had halted with *H.Q.* and the *3rd* and *17th Cavalry Brigades* in Beaulieu and the *18th Brigade* in Ognolles.

The duty assigned to the leading cavalry division of *H.K.K.II.* in the advance was the penetration of the dense forest on the east bank of the Oise. An early start was essential in view of the distance to be covered and the probability of delays. The *18th Brigade* left Ognolles at 2 a.m., and the Division pushed on from Beaulieu at 3 a.m., with the *3rd Brigade* acting as advanced guard. Marching southwards the Division soon reached Lassigny, from which town all the inhabitants had fled after locking up their houses and stables. Here a halt was made to water the horses, but this proved a difficult and lengthy operation as the water supply was far from plentiful. The men were more fortunate, as quantities of peaches were found in the gardens. The Division then headed for the Oise at Thourotte. After crossing the heights at Lassigny the aspect of the country gradually altered as the wooded hills bordering the Oise were neared. The day grew very hot as the column pressed forward. Moving down the valley of the Matz, the Oise was reached at 10 a.m., and the river was crossed by the wooden suspension bridge at Thourotte beneath the chateau of le Plessis Brion. To shorten the column the regimental and first line transport and the light ammunition column were left behind when the Oise was crossed, a decision that was to be bitterly regretted the next day. At first an easterly direction was maintained as the regiments traversed the glades of the beautiful Forest of Laigue, but after reaching the middle of this great woodland tract the line of advance bent south-eastwards and about 2 p.m. the division halted at Offemont. Here, close to the ruins of the old Monastery, with its crumbling towers brooding over the placid carp ponds that were set like jewels amid the park and gardens, the division rested in the shade for three hours, horses were watered and fed and the men had a meal and a bathe in the ponds.

At 5 p.m. the march was resumed but only at a walk. The division now headed south-westwards, for General von der Marwitz, who had been at Offemont with the *4th Division*, had altered his direction of advance and was heading for Nanteuil le Haudouin in accordance with the information he had received at 4 p.m. (*Vide supra p. 315.*) Marwitz, before leaving to join the *2nd Division*, ordered the *4th Division* to move by St. Jean aux Bois and Gilocourt.

At dusk the Aisne was crossed at Rethondes and then the division at once plunged into the even larger and denser Forest of Compiegne. Hour after hour passed as the long column wended its way under the trees in the darkness, no clearing appeared although an occasional deserted farm came into sight and was passed by, or one of the small scattered villages was traversed. There were numerous short halts, but despite these men gradually fell asleep on their tired horses, and then woke up some time later to find themselves in a different squadron or among an unfamiliar regiment. Lances dropped from tired hands and fell clattering to the ground,[1] the horses showed signs of exhaustion, but still the advance went on. Midnight found the Division passing to the south of St. Jean aux Bois, approaching the southern edge of the vast woodland. Gradually the trees got thinner, the column passed out into the open, and moved down the winding road into Gilocourt. Then turning westward it moved down the Automne valley and about 4 a.m., on the 1st September the main body reached Bethisy St. Martin. Here a fairly long halt was made, the rear brigade halting in the neighbouring village of Bethisy St. Pierre about half a mile to the north.

Plans for the 1st September.

From the information that had come to hand, Kluck realised that Lanrezac was falling back and the B.E.F. was retiring southward from the line of the Oise between Noyon and Verberie, whilst Maunoury was withdrawing towards Clermont. He determined, therefore, to attack the retiring B.E.F. during the 1st, and he ordered a pursuit in a southerly direction. The *IV Reserve Corps* was to continue its advance, covering the right flank and communications of the *First Army*, the *II Corps* would cross the Oise about Verberie and reconnoitre towards the line Clermont—Creil—Senlis, the *IV Corps* would move right through the Forest of Compiegne, the *III Corps* would advance to the line Taillefontaine—Vivieres, the *18th Division (IX Corps)* would march to Longpont, whilst the *17th Division* made a forced march and closed up to Champs. Thus it will be seen that Kluck had once more altered direction, and that the bait offered by the B.E.F. had diverted him from his previous objective—Lanrezac's open left flank. Kluck recognised this, for he actually ordered *H.K.K.II.* to move through Villers Cotterets against the French flank. It is clear, however, that Kluck when

---

[1] In 1914 all lance-corporals and privates in the German Cavalry were armed with the lance, sword, and carbine.

Bayonets were not issued to the Cavalry until the end of 1914, and in July, 1915, the swords were withdrawn. During 1916 a number of regiments acting as divisional cavalry (chiefly *Reserve* and *Ersatz* formations) were converted into dismounted rifle regiments (*Schützen Regimenter*). The men of these units were then armed and equipped as infantrymen. (*Handbook of the German Army in War, April, 1918, p. 64.*)

he issued this order had not heard of Marwitz's southward swing towards Nanteuil, and good though the order might be, yet under the circumstances it could lead to no co-operation at all with Bülow.

Meanwhile *H.K.K.I.* had received orders to advance on the 1st through the wooded country between Soissons and Villers Cotterets. But Richthofen's divisions did not even cross the Aisne, whilst the *Second Army* on the same day advanced slowly to the line of the Oise—Aisne canal.

On the French side Lanrezac seized the opportunity to withdraw his army beyond the Aisne, and thus by nightfall had almost escaped from the dangerous situation in which he stood. On the other flank of the B.E.F. Maunoury's Army was still holding from Clermont to Senlis, with its right wing swung back through the Forest of Halatte, south of the Oise.

During the 31st G.H.Q. considered that the German forces had completed their westerly movement and were pivoting round to the south and south-east, covered by at least two cavalry divisions which had reached the Oise during the afternoon. The orders for the 1st to the B.E.F. were that the retirement would be continued, the I Corps moving to la Ferté Milon—Betz, the II Corps to Nanteuil, and the III Corps to Baron. The rear would be covered by the Cavalry Division.

A NIGHT OF RUMOURS.

The engagement at night on the Croix St. Ouen road, when the *9th Cavalry Division* collided with the outposts of the 4th Division, showed clearly that the latter's position was really exposed and that the enemy had once more established definite contact. Naturally the desire was to open the retirement of the exposed III Corps as early as possible on the 1st, but even by 10 p.m. all the troops had not arrived and a very early start was out of the question. It was clear that if the III Corps was attacked strongly at dawn—and no one could be certain what the fighting in the forest during the darkness really heralded—then the gap existing between the III and II Corps constituted a real danger. But once the III Corps could withdraw from the the Oise valley this gap could easily be lessened by the two corps inclining inwards; until, however, it was decreased, it was a constant source of anxiety. For the moment the outer flank of the 4th Division appeared to be well covered, for not only did it rest on the Oise but, at the time when the division reached Verberie, the bridge was held by a chasseur battalion. But even this security had vanished before midnight, for when the G.S.O. I of the division went down at about 11 p.m. to the bridge he found that the chasseurs had been withdrawn and that this flank was open; and as in rear of the division there stretched the great masses of the forest in which the Germans had already established themselves, the position of the 4th Division might well cause its commander considerable anxiety. This anxiety was heightened by disquieting proofs of the proximity and activity of the pursuers. Earlier that evening, about 6 p.m., a German aeroplane flew over the bivouac of the Howitzer Brigade (XXXVII R.F.A.) of the 4th Division on the plateau above Verberie and fired a light. Then later there had been the outpost collision in the forest to the north of Verberie. The situation of the division had suddenly become grave.

In Nery, however, only three miles away, the general feeling that evening was one of safety. The villagers were quite ignorant of the enemy's whereabouts, and although for days they had heard wild, alarmist, and impossible rumours, yet the natural inclination had been to disbelieve any report. Thus on this very evening when a farm labourer rode into the village and announced that the Germans were coming on and that the Forest of Compiegne was black with them, no one would listen to him. With one accord the villagers shouted; "That's rubbish!" *(C'est de la blague!)* The bearer of bad news, merely jeered at for his warning, then passed sorrowfully away to the southward and was soon swallowed up in the growing darkness. But nevertheless the situation at Nery was precarious. Nor were signs wanting that it was so, although naturally they were not known at Nery. At about 2 a.m. the crash of a sudden outburst of close-range rifle fire rang down the streets at Saintines where the 19th Infantry Brigade was billeted. Three *Uhlans*, undoubtedly a patrol sent out by the *9th Uhlans* part of the advanced guard of the *4th Cavalry Division* had got into the place and opened fire. Then amidst the general confusion they made their escape in the darkness. Nor was this all. Early in the morning, about 4 a.m., a civilian saw a long column of cavalry

and guns passing through Bethisy, and recognised their helmets as Germans. (It was the *4th Cavalry Division.*) Unfortunately the information was sent on only to the II Corps at Crepy, instead of to the III Corps at Verberie. The II Corps duly passed on the report to G.H.Q. at Dammartin and requested that it might be transmitted to the III Corps. But the information only came to hand after heavy firing had already been heard. Thus the short summer night passed. What was in store for the B.E.F. when dawn broke?

A DAY OF ALARMS, 1ST SEPTEMBER.

Sketch 3.

Not one of the British corps got away scatheless on this day. In the I Corps the blow fell heaviest on the 2nd Division. The advanced guard of the *6th Division (III Corps)* overtook the British rearguard in the morning, and a long severe action was fought at close quarters around Rond de la Reine in the Forest of Villers Cotterets. The Germans gradually advanced as the day wore on, and it was not until 6 p.m. that the British got clear away. The *6th Division* pushed on and reached Villers Cotterets that night. Further to the west the 3rd Cavalry Brigade was engaged with the advanced guard of the *5th Division (III Corps)* near Taillefontaine and was not able to shake off the pursuers until after midday. The *5th Division* marched forward that evening to Vauciennes.

In the II Corps it was the British 5th Division that was engaged. About 6 a.m. its outpost line was attacked by Marwitz's five *Jäger* battalions which had come up after a magnificent forced march, and the *Jäger* were supported by the *10th Hussars*, Corps Cavalry of the *IV Corps*. By 10 a.m. the action was developing into a serious fight, for the German advanced guards were gradually closing up to the scene of action. But fortunately the necessary time had been gained, as the fighting at Nery was over, and the 5th Division at once set about breaking off the fight and opening its retirement. Directly the division was clear of Crepy it was only followed for some distance by cavalry patrols. The *IV Corps* reached Crepy that night.

But it was on the left flank that the principal interest centred on the 1st September. On receipt of III Corps Orders, the 4th

Division at 2 a.m. issued its orders. The columns and trains were to start at 4 a.m., whilst the division and the 19th Infantry Brigade were to be ready to march at 7 a.m., and as far as Raray two roads would be used. On reaching Raray one column would be formed for the rest of the march to Baron, and from Raray to Baron the 19th Infantry Brigade and the XXXII Brigade R.F.A., would act as rearguard. The columns and trains started on their march punctually, and at the same time the divisional commander, realising that his headquarters at Verberie were situated in a hole, and growing more and more uneasy about the general situation, moved up on to the plateau together with his C.R.A. General Snow had just previously issued instructions to the rear brigade about its action in case of sudden attack and the line that must be held. It was on the plateau, between 6.30 and 7 a.m., that a report reached General Snow that the 1st Cavalry Brigade had been attacked at Nery.

Meanwhile during the morning the *2nd Cavalry Division* had been despatched to attack St. Sauveur from the east. The village was held by the two rearguard battalions (1/Somerset L.I. and 1/Rifle Brigade) of the 11th Infantry Brigade. There was a prolonged fire fight, but the German cavalry failed to enter the village until after the rearguard had been withdrawn, on the general retirement being eventually resumed on this part of the front. One other battalion (1/Hants) of the 11th Brigade was also sharply engaged during the morning with the *Hussar Brigade*. The *2nd Cavalry Division* then halted without crossing the valley of the Automne. Marwitz had decided that in face of the resistance that had been unexpectedly encountered and being out of touch with his *4th Division*, it would be wiser to await the arrival of the *II Corps*, now approaching Verberie, before committing his two divisions more deeply.

Actually in front of Verberie there was no serious attack on the 1st September. The *9th Cavalry Division* remained about Croix St. Ouen, where it had come to a standstill after its failure the night before. It pushed a strong patrol, however, through Verberie, and Sergeant J. Fenton, R.E., the Intelligence Clerk of the III Corps who had been left with a bicycle at Villeneuve to collect any messages that might arrive there for his headquarters, which had already moved back to Raray, saw a German cavalry patrol riding southward from Verberie. At that moment there were no troops between him and the German cavalry, and he realised that if he remained where he was, then the only message that he would receive would be in German. Consequently he cycled back to Corps headquarters to report what he had observed. But apparently this activity was all that the *9th Cavalry Division* was capable of on the 1st September and it signally failed to harass the retirement of the III Corps later in the day or to keep in touch with it.

After this brief summary of what happened on the 1st on the rest of the British front, we can now recount in detail the fight at Nery and the adventures of the *4th Cavalry Division* on this fateful day.

PART II. THE CHANCE ENCOUNTER.

NERY.

"It is so still where sleeps the little town,
White in its woods, and on the easy hill,
Drab with crisp stubble, where one crooked clown
Reaps the last ridge of gold, it is so still."

F. Taylor.

Sketch 4.

The little village of Nery, of less than six hundred inhabitants, lies on an old Roman road. The village is perched near the top of the western bank of a tiny stream[1] which, running northwards, cuts its small but deep valley between two plateaux, both of some command and with fairly abrupt escarpments overlooking the river bed. The village is commanded by the plateau on the eastern side, and the eastern escarpment is considerably steeper than that to the west of the valley. South of the village the valley head was a thickly wooded ravine, blind and overgrown with bushes; but below Feu Farm the bottom widened, and here abreast of the village the steep slope to the west was fairly clear, though the eastern side was dotted with bushes and scattered trees, and on this plateau there were also two or three copses. The valley itself had been selected to carry part of the new railway that was to connect Paris and Compiegne, but in 1914 no work had been started on it in the vicinity of Nery. The village, as the photographs show, stood in a somewhat commanding position and the church spire was an undoubted landmark. The houses themselves, though small, were well built with stout garden walls of stone or brick. To the south of the village in a dominating position, there was a large sugar factory, another conspicuous and easily recognised feature of the landscape. To the south-east, but partly buried in a branch valley was Feu Farm, a substantial building with the usual sheds and outhouses. The fields around the village produced crops of beet and corn, but the latter had just been cut and stood in stooks waiting to be carried.

We left the *4th Cavalry Division* in the Automne Valley, halted in the two villages of Bethisy. Here three abandoned British

---

[1] In September this stream was nearly dry.

NERY.   Looking from above Feu Farm.

NERY.   Looking east towards the German Position from L. Battery Field.

lorries were found, and all ranks succeeded in getting either bread from the derelict supply wagons or cakes from the houses. The people had at first thought that their visitors were British and brought out to them hot drinks that proved very acceptable, but only too soon they discovered that the intruders were Germans. From the inhabitants it was easily ascertained that the British had left the villages about a couple of hours earlier. One, however, remained, a slumbering British sentry, and he suddenly awoke to learn that, so far as he was concerned, the war was over.

The morning broke grey, and at first a dense September mist shrouded the countryside in an almost impenetrable veil, the obvious forerunner of a scorching day. But at about 4 a.m., when the march was restarted, the morning mists were beginning to rise from the Automne valley. Slowly the long column climbed up the winding road on the left bank. On reaching the top of the plateau patrols were at once sent out to reconnoitre. Meanwhile the rest of the column dismounted, and, pending the return of the patrols, the men lay down on the dusty road in preference to stretching themselves on the dew-soaked grass, whilst the tired horses nibbled at the grass by the roadside or pulled oats from the stooks that were stacked in the reaped fields near the road.

It was now decided to relieve the *3rd Brigade* which had so far acted as advanced guard, and the *17th Brigade* was detailed for this duty when the march was resumed a few minutes later. An officer's patrol of the *18th Dragoons* was immediately sent out in the direction of Rozieres. Almost directly after it had started, at about 5 a.m., a patrol of the *17th Dragoons* rode in and reported that a British force was bivouacking at Nery and was resting there uncovered and unsuspecting. This was too good a chance to lose. An order was at once issued to deploy in the direction of Nery. No doubt it was assumed that the *2nd* and *9th Divisions* were in the vicinity and would co-operate when the firing opened. The advanced guard brigade, *17th*, was given the duty of covering the left flank and it was also responsible for the protection of the guns which were coming into action immediately on its right. So far little could be seen of the village in the heavy mist that still swathed the plateau. Only a few scattered houses and the church spire could be dimly made out standing on a hill. To the south-west the loom of a massive building was just visible, the sugar factory, but of the bivouac mentioned in the report there was as yet no sign.

So far in Nery itself there was no suspicion at all of the immediate danger that was impending. At 3.15 a.m., however, Major R. J. P. Anderson, 11th Hussars, went down into the lines and saw 2nd Lieut. G. W. A. Tailby who was to take out a patrol to reconnoitre the eastern heights. He ordered 2nd Lieut. Tailby to leave the village by the north-eastern exit, then to make for the eastern plateau, take a sweep to the south, and thus make good the whole front of the brigade.[1] He was ordered to notice any hostile movement to the northwards, and he was warned that he might run into French piquets. Both the 5th Dragoon Guards and Queen's Bays also sent out patrols to the north and south of the village, but these two patrols returned in due course and reported that they had encountered no signs of an enemy. The third patrol was to have a very different experience.

2nd Lieut. Tailby's patrol consisted of a corporal and five men. As ordered by Major Anderson, the patrol climbed to the top of the eastern plateau, and, after riding southwards, moved along the southern and eastern sides. The mist was very thick and visibility was limited to about a hundred yards. 2nd Lieut. Tailby had almost completed the circuit of the plateau and was about a mile from Nery when the mist slightly cleared away, and there about a hundred and fifty yards off he saw a column of cloaked and helmeted cavalry, the men dismounted in sections, and in a flash recognised them as Germans.[2] Fortunately the enemy had so far not observed the British patrol, but the latter was not fated to get away unnoticed. At this moment one of the patrol, in an excess of zeal, jumped off his horse and opened fire on the German cavalry. An order rang out, and the Dragoons sprang into their saddles as the patrol swung round and galloped off. The enemy, however, barred the direct line of retreat to Nery, so at first 2nd Lieut. Tailby led his men to the north-eastward in the hope of shaking off the pursuit in the

---

[1] It was his first patrol, and it was destined to be a memorable one. His full report is given in *The Attack on the 1st Cavalry Brigade at Nery*, by General T. T. Pitman, C.B. (*Cavalry Journal*, April, 1920).

[2] Part of the *Dragoon Brigade* that was just taking over advanced guard to the *4th Division*.

mist. With the enemy thundering behind them the patrol reached the crest of the plateau and there fortunately struck a rough cart-track leading down from the ridge. Racing down this 2nd Lieut. Tailby's horse put his foot in a hole and turned head over heels. By the time he had regained his horse and remounted the German cavalry had decided to give up the chase and had begun to retire. The patrol then galloped on down the hill, the one essential being to reach Nery and to report the surprising information that had been obtained. Outside an estaminet, at the foot of the hill, 2nd Lieut. Tailby saw a German cloak and a rifle, and a woman told him that three Germans had just bolted from the house. The cloak was secured to prove the presence of German cavalry, and asking the way on to the Bethisy—Nery road, 2nd Lieut. Tailby and his patrol soon reached the village. On arrival at Nery the corporal was sent to warn the 5th Dragoon Guards, who unfortunately did not believe the information, and 2nd Lieut. Tailby at once went to Colonel Pitman to report what had happened. It was nearly 5.30 a.m.

Meanwhile the 1st Cavalry Brigade at Nery had been ordered overnight to be ready to continue the retirement southward at 4.30 a.m. on the 1st. But at that hour, owing to the heavy morning mist, it was impossible to see objects more than two hundred yards away. The units, however, fell in at 4.30 a.m., and were then ordered to stand fast until 5 a.m., whilst the posts holding the edge of the village remained in position. At 5 a.m. the men fell out to get breakfast and a message was received that the march had been temporarily postponed. In most of the other units, with the exception of the 11th Hussars, as the horses had been saddled up in the dark the saddles were shifted.

"L" Battery had been halted in mass in its field at the southern end of the village. The poles were now let down and arrangements were made to water the horses by sections at the sugar factory, whilst the men had their breakfasts. The Battery Commander seized the opportunity to proceed to Brigade Headquarters so as to receive further orders.

This was the comparatively peaceful state of affairs in the village, whilst on the eastern heights under cover of the mist a devastating storm was brewing.

THE ATTACK.

On receiving 2nd Lieut. Tailby's information, Colonel Pitman at once went to Brigade Headquarters to report to General Briggs what had been discovered by his patrol; and Major Anderson immediately proceeded to get the 11th Hussars into position along the eastern edge of the village. Colonel Pitman had just returned to his regiment when the firing broke out.

It was 5.40 a.m.,[1] and at Brigade Headquarters there were assembled the Brigadier (Brig.-Genl. C. J. Briggs, C.B.), the Brigade Major (Major J. S. Cawley),[2] and the Battery Commander (Major the Hon. W. D. Sclater-Booth). Suddenly with a rending crash, a high explosive shell burst over the village and was followed by a heavy, prolonged outburst of rifle and machine-gun fire from the eastern plateau.

Confirmation of the accuracy of the report was at once attainable, for one of the first shell fired went through the roof of Brigade Headquarters, and General Briggs picked up the time-fuze, saw that it was set for 800 metres, and that it was German. It was necessary to warn neighbouring commanders who would have been alarmed by this outburst of heavy, concentrated fire, and who would have difficulty in locating the scene of the engagement in the heavy mist. Motor-cyclists, therefore, were sent at once to warn General Allenby (Cavalry Division) and General Snow (4th Division) that the 1st Cavalry Brigade had been attacked by German cavalry, strength unknown.

When the action opened, General Briggs thought that his brigade had been attacked by a comparatively weak body of German cavalry that was wandering behind the general outpost line; and, under these circumstances, as the village of Nery was small General Briggs considered that the 5th Dragoon Guards was not necessary for its defence. Consequently he ordered Colonel Pitman to extend the front of his regiment so as to include that part originally occupied by the 5th Dragoon Guards and thus release it. At the same time the Brigadier ordered Colonel Pitman to detail one squadron of his regiment to act as a brigade reserve, and A Squadron was selected for this duty. General Briggs then gave Lieut.-Colonel

---
[1] From a note made at the time by an officer of the 11th Hussars.
[2] Major Cawley was killed in the fight.

G. K. Ansell, commanding the 5th Dragoon Guards, a free hand to act mounted against the flank and rear of the German cavalry.

So far as could be ascertained at the moment the volume of fire appeared to be directed on the exposed portions of the 1st Cavalry Brigade, "L" Battery and the Queen's Bays. The terrified horses of the Queen's Bays broke loose in panic; and whilst most of them galloped off across the open country, a small mob swept up the village street and then dispersed across the open. "L" Battery was even more unfortunate.[1] Captain E. K. Bradbury and the subalterns were standing near the hay-stacks in the north-west corner of the field when a shell burst over the battery and immediately the whole field was swept by a devastating fire. The poles being down, the teams had no chance, and as the horses tried to bolt the poles were driven into the ground and the field rapidly became a shambles.[2] It was a moment that called for a leader, and Bradbury rose magnificently to the occasion. Shouting for volunteers, he raced for the guns followed by the three subalterns and by Sergeant D. Nelson. The officers, assisted by some men who were helping with the horses, managed to unlimber three of the guns and turn them in the direction of the enemy. Captain Bradbury took one, Lieut. Giffard another, and Lieuts. Campbell and Munday the third. But the ammunition wagons were twenty yards away and over this death-swept space the rounds had to be carried up to the guns.

Unfortunately a disaster occurred at once for, before it could fire a round, Lieut.-Campbell's gun was knocked out by a direct hit. The two officers then ran over to Captain Bradbury's gun and reinforced his detachment. The two guns opened fire at once on the enemy, but Lieut. Giffard's gun, after firing a very few rounds, was smothered with shells, Lieut. Giffard was severely wounded and nearly all the detachment were either killed or wounded. Thus only Bradbury's gun still remained in action, and round this gathered the few survivors from the other two guns,

---

[1] When the firing opened, Major Sclater-Booth at once left Brigade Headquarters to return to his battery. As he was attempting to cross the beetfield, behind the battery's bivouac, he was blown down by a shell that burst just in front of him and remained lying there unconscious until about 11 a.m., and here he was found by the Rear Party, who brought him in just before the position was evacuated.

[2] The Battery lost 150 horses out of its war establishment of 228.

and the detachment was further reinforced by Battery-Sergeant-Major G. T. Dorrell. This gun bore a charmed life, and, despite a constant stream of casualties, Captain Bradbury kept it in action against the three hostile batteries under a thousand yards away. As the detachment dwindled and the difficulty of getting up ammunition became greater, fire became desultory. But for well over an hour the grim, unequal duel continued of the one gun against the twelve, until at last, as he was trying to fetch up more ammunition, Bradbury was mortally wounded. The detachment now consisted of only two men, both wounded, B.S.M. Dorrell and Sergt. Nelson. Gradually the few rounds of ammunition at the gun were expended and then the end came—the gun was silent at last, but it still stood there unconquered, glaring defiantly at the foe. It had, however, done its task, for it had attracted much of the enemy's attention and fire during the difficult part of the action, reinforcements were now arriving, and the crisis was nearly overpast.[1]

Behind "L" the machine-gun section of the Bays under Lieut. A. J. R. Lamb, had been brought into action at once at the southern end of the village and the guns opened a telling fire. At the same time one N.C.O. and two men of the Bays moved down and occupied the sugar factory so as to secure this flank still further. Meanwhile the 11th Hussars had occupied the walls along the eastern edge of Nery and at once opened a brisk rifle fire against the Germans. The Hussars machine-gun section, under 2nd Lieut. D. McMurrough Kavanagh, was brought into action just to the east of the church. Almost immediately afterwards, to the eastward, a squadron loomed up dimly through the mist. Just as the machine guns were about to open on this inviting target within five hundred yards, the French interpreter intervened and declared that the horsemen were French. The squadron moved southward, disappeared in the mist, and the opportunity had passed away. Later on the German cavalry appeared to be working round to

---
[1] Of the detachments, Captain E. K. Bradbury was mortally wounded, and died at the gun, Lieut. J. D. Campbell was killed, Lieut. L. F. H. Munday died of his wounds on 3rd September, and Lieut. J. Giffard, B.S.M. Dorrell, and Sergt. Nelson were all wounded.
The Victoria Cross was awarded to Captain Bradbury (posthumously), to B.S.M. Dorrell, and to Sergt. Nelson for their courage and devotion at Nery.
Sergt. (then Lieut. and a/Major) D. Nelson died of wounds on the 8th April, 1918.

the south of the village and threatening the right flank of the brigade. To strengthen the southern defences, therefore, the machine guns were moved to the south-east corner, and from this point they opened fire at once on the German batteries under seven hundred yards away, sweeping up and down the gun line with considerable effect. On the left flank of the Hussars fire had been opened at 900 yards and gradually reduced to 650. At this range it was very accurate and completely stopped the German attack, but there is no doubt that the sting had already been taken out of it by Colonel Ansell's counter-attack, which is described later.

In the 5th Dragoon Guards the men ran to their horses directly the firing broke out, and thus any serious stampede was prevented, though this part of the village was not subjected to the same heavy fire as the unprotected bivouacs at the southern end. On receiving General Briggs's order to attack the German right flank, Colonel Ansell ordered C Squadron to occupy and hold the houses and walls at the north-eastern end of Nery and thus secure this flank. He then personally led out A and B squadrons on a wide sweep to the north, so as to outflank the German right and thus take the extreme pressure off the open southern flank. Having seen Colonel Ansell start on his mission, General Briggs walked back along the line from north to south.

To cover the attack of the *4th Cavalry Division* the three horse artillery batteries, with the *Guard Machine-Gun Battery* on their left, unlimbered in a long line on the edge of the ravine between five and six hundred yards from the eastern edge of the village. Under cover of their fire, the *3rd Cavalry Brigade* was to advance from the direction of Bethisy, against the British left, the attack against the other flank being entrusted to the *17th Cavalry Brigade*. In this brigade the *18th Dragoons* was to be deployed for the attack whilst the *17th Dragoons* was held back at le Plessis Chatelain, partly to act as a support and partly to cover the open left flank. The *18th Cavalry Brigade* was kept in hand as a divisional reserve, and its two Hussar regiments formed up in squadron columns in the valleys and hollows behind the centre of the line. As soon as the guns unlimbered they opened a heavy and devastating fire on the exposed bivouacs of the Queen's Bays and "L" Battery.

Then a few minutes later the whole of the *Guard Machine-Gun Battery* came into action and swept with withering bursts of fire the now confused and struggling mass in the open bivouacs to the south of the village.

The officer's patrol that was proceeding to Rozieres was still close to Nery when the action opened. The officer in charge saw the confusion caused by the sudden outburst of close-range fire and noticed that small parties had begun drifting away south-westward along the Rully road. He ordered his patrol (six men) to open fire on these fugitives, but without much result. The effect of the surprise, however, soon passed away in the absence of any immediate attempt to rush the position. The defence hardened, a few resolute men took charge and reorganised a really effective resistance, guns were brought into action, the outskirts of the village were occupied, machine guns opened up from points of vantage, and a counter-attack was delivered. The *4th Cavalry Division* had stumbled on a hornet's nest.

The attack by the German right against the north-eastern end of Nery was entrusted to the *3rd Brigade, 9th Uhlans* and *3rd Cuirassiers*, the former regiment being on the right. Just as this attack was starting Colonel Ansell's two squadrons swept up and drove home a counter-attack against the right of the German line. The *3rd Brigade* came to a standstill and a fire fight broke out. Doubtless the mist hid not the strength but the weakness of Colonel Ansell's force, and the German line suffering somewhat heavily the British numbers were exaggerated. Colonel Ansell unfortunately was killed, and then came the time to withdraw, before the force was overwhelmed by sheer weight of numbers. Great gallantry was shown in the bold handling of the small parties which covered the retirement. On the outer flank one sergeant galloped forward with his troop to within a hundred yards of the *9th Uhlans*, and then dismounted his men and opened rapid fire. This not only caused the Germans heavy casualties on this flank, but also it threw the Uhlan line into considerable confusion, thus enabling the main body and the covering parties to be withdrawn without any serious loss. This prompt, bold, and well-conceived *riposte* threw the *3rd Brigade* on to the defensive for the rest of the day and materially assisted in the successful defence of Nery.

On the southern flank the *17th Brigade* had dismounted as the bombardment opened, and two squadrons on the extreme left flank of the Division at once advanced to attack the southern end of the village, the other squadron being kept back in support and merely pushing forward a strong patrol under an officer towards the sugar factory. One troop, from Major G. H. A. Ing's squadron of the Bays, pushed out towards the sugar factory. The troop leader, Lieut. C. N. Champion de Crespigny, was killed, but the sergeant-major (Fraser) handled the men boldly and succeeded for a time in stemming the German advance in this direction. The party was finally shelled out of the factory.

The German guns continued firing with undiminished violence, and covered by this bombardment the squadrons advanced by rushes against the village, but the defence was stubborn and the fire of the defenders was accurate and deadly, it tore gaps in the ranks of the assailants and several of the leaders were shot. It was not to be the easy victory that had been expected at first. Gradually the advance came to a standstill after the dismounted cavalry had reached within a few hundred yards of their goal. The assailants could not cross the head of the valley, and a brisk fire-fight broke out. Any prolongation of the action was by no means in favour of the German cavalry. At any moment reinforcements might reach the British, and the division was bound to economise its ammunition, as its ammunition column had been left behind in the forest of Laigue. Suddenly, while the fire fight was at its height, a body of horsemen formed for attack and galloping at full speed appeared right behind the firing line of the *18th Dragoons*. Fortunately it was only the *18th Cavalry Brigade* moving forward in support, and finding difficulty in keeping direction in the mist. The Brigade Major of the *17th Brigade* luckily succeeded in bringing the advancing squadrons to a halt before they crashed into the rear of the firing line.

It is now time to turn to the advance of the *18th Brigade* and see what had occasioned this diversion. In order to relieve the *3rd* and *17th Brigades*, which were suffering considerable losses and had both come to a standstill, the *16th Hussars* was ordered to deliver a mounted attack and override all resistance at the southern end of Nery. The attack was led by the Brigadier, Colonel von

Printz, in person. His orders were, "Form up and charge! Follow me!" Lieut.-Colonel Ludendorff who like all his officers had been unable, owing to the mist, to get any clear view of the ground, asked whether any ground reconnaissance should be made. The orderly officer of the Brigade promptly answered, "Certainly, during the advance," but under the conditions this was impossible. The Regiment formed at once for attack in four waves, with the *4th Squadron* in the van. After galloping about five hundred yards a sunken road suddenly loomed up and crossing it with tired horses caused considerable disorder. So far the Regiment in its advance had suffered little from the British fire, no doubt owing to the indistinct target it offered in the mist. Even such shell and bullets as fell among it were probably only overs really fired at the gun line or at the *18th Dragoons*. After crossing the road the Hussars galloped on, but the ground now became very difficult and after a thousand yards had been traversed a deep blind ravine, overgrown with thorn bushes, was encountered. It was an obstacle impossible to charge across, nor was any path through it to be seen. A few men, mounted on specially trained horses, plunged down the side of the ravine, but they all fell and the attempt was not repeated. In front of this unexpected natural obstacle the charge came to an abrupt conclusion, the regiment being still about seven hundred yards away from the village. Mounted action being impracticable the leading squadron dismounted and the men took their carbines, but then it was ascertained that the other three squadrons were missing. At this moment, it must have been about 8 a.m., a hostile battery was observed unlimbering to the westward.[1] The led horses of the Hussars were quite unprotected and it appeared to be impossible to advance, and so Colonel Ludendorff regretfully ordered his men to remount and retire. Owing to the mist, and to the fact that "I" opened fire on the line of the German guns, this withdrawal was carried out without many casualties. Even as the Hussars fell back no sign of the missing squadrons was observed, but, when Colonel Ludendorff reported to General von Garnier, the regimental commander was informed that the three squadrons had been kept back by the Divisional General for his own use. The mounted attack of course had been a failure, but

---

[1] The 2 sections of "I" Battery, R.H.A., under Captain H. P. Burnyeat.

it possibly did divert attention for a few moments from other parts of a sorely tried line.

The *15th Hussars* also attacked at the same time as its sister regiment the *16th*. Formed up in squadron columns, in hollows, the *15th Hussars* advanced on the right of the *16th* and with its right flank just to the south of the German gun line. With two squadrons in the first wave, one in the second wave, and a fourth echeloned to the right rear, a mounted attack was launched at the gallop. The regiment advancing through beetfields suffered severely from fire delivered from the front of the village, but being fortunate enough to strike the eastern side of the valley, where the descent was easier than at the ravine head near Feu Farm, the *15th* reached the bottom of the valley. Here the men dismounted and took their carbines to continue the advance on foot, prolonging the right flank of the *18th Dragoons*. But British reinforcements were now rapidly and visibly reaching Nery from all sides, and not only was the situation of the *4th Cavalry Division* becoming critical but its ammunition was running short. Further, during the action, General von Garnier had heard of British troops both at Bethisy and at Crepy. The General determined, therefore, to break off the fight and to retire at once in an easterly direction.

Before this decision had been forced on General von Garnier, an officer's patrol sent out by the *1st Squadron* of the *18th Dragoons* had pushed on to the sugar factory, and on entering it found that it had been evacuated by the British. The patrol leader decided to push on, but at that moment a small party of British Cavalry was sighted to the west of the Rully road. The Germans opened fire on it and it withdrew.[1] Immediately afterwards in the same direction the patrol saw the flat khaki caps of the British showing up, at first singly but then in ever increasing numbers. The commander of the patrol at once extended his men and opened fire. But the numbers of the advancing infantry rapidly increased and soon threatened to outflank the *18th Dragoons*. This development was reported to the brigadier, but only small reinforcements could be sent forward, and the danger grew apace. The position of the led horses was threatened and they had to be moved. The *17th*

---

[1] This was probably the advance of Lieut. Heath's troop, which is described on page 338.

Dragoons had already been brought up to cover the open flank of the guns, which were now themselves endangered. Further the ammunition was almost exhausted, the guns had nearly expended what they carried with them, and so far as rifle ammunition went hardly any of the dismounted men had more than a few rounds left. It was impossible to continue the action much longer. The situation was momentarily growing more critical. The sudden attack on the 1st Cavalry Brigade had failed, and the position of the *4th Cavalry Division* was rapidly becoming extremely dangerous.

Arrival of the British reinforcements
and the close of the action.

It is now time to consider the principal reinforcements that moved to the assistance of the hard pressed Brigade at Nery, their action, and their effect on the result of the fight.

The headquarters of the Cavalry Division had billeted overnight at St. Waast[1] (immediately to the south of Verberie). Just as the G.O.C. left his billet he was informed of the attack on his 1st Cavalry Brigade. He at once moved with the 4th Cavalry Brigade and "I" Battery, R.H.A., towards Nery, and at 7 a.m., whilst on the march, he was met by the Staff Captain of the 1st Cavalry Brigade. The mist made it very difficult to see what was actually happening, but from the report he now received General Allenby decided that the best way to help was by a turning movement from the south. Consequently he deployed part of his force to the south of the Roman Road, having previously pushed one squadron further to the southward so that it should work down the valley from that direction. "I" Battery was ordered into action, and Cavalry Divisional Headquarters was established about three quarters of a mile west of the sugar factory.

With "I" Battery, R.H.A. (Major W. G. Thompson), was one section of "D" R.H.A. which had become attached to "I" during the retreat from le Cateau. Major Thompson had then temporarily organised the eight guns into two four-gun batteries, taking com-

---

[1] St. Waast (and its variants, St. Vaast, St. Vast, and Domvast) found as a component in so many place names in the departments of Manche, Nord, Oise, Pas de Calais, Seine Inferieure, Somme, etc., commemorates the name of a fifth century bishop of Arras — Vedastus.

mand of one himself and placing the other under Captain H. P. Burnyeat. On receiving orders to come into action, Major Thompson selected for Captain Burnyeat's four guns a semi-concealed position to the south of the Roman Road and about two thousand yards away from the German batteries.

"L" had just fired its last round, the German firing line was closing in on Nery, and some of our wounded could be seen coming back from the village. But, a more welcome sight was the appearance further back of some advancing infantry, in shirt sleeves (Warwickshire and Dublin Fusiliers)—their appearance being due to a hasty parade. Leaving Captain Burnyeat to open fire, Major Thompson rode away southward to find another position for his own guns, but unfortunately he had not succeeded in this when the action terminated almost as suddenly as it had begun.

There was some delay and it was not until about 8 a.m., nearly half an hour after Major Thompson left, that Captain Burnyeat got his guns into action. From the position occupied the German gun line was almost enfiladed. Despite the mist which still hung about Captain Burnyeat could make out the opposite ridge, and the factory chimney fortunately provided a convenient and distinct aiming point. The battery opened fire and its effectiveness was immediately apparent. One of the German batteries at once swung round to engage "I" and the pressure on Nery was sensibly relieved. By chance the German battery commander was misled by the pole of a derelict cultivator that happened to be sticking up in the air near Captain Burnyeat's guns. Dimly seen through the mist this pole seems to have been mistaken for an observation ladder in the battery position, and a heavy, and fortunately an extremely accurate, fire was concentrated on it, with the happiest possible result so far as "I" was concerned. As well as being under "I"'s well-burst shrapnel, the German guns were swept by heavy bursts of fire from the machine-gun sections of the Bays and of the 11th Hussars.

It will be remembered that the 4th Cavalry Brigade had accompanied General Allenby when he moved across towards Nery. The Brigade, preceded by the 2nd Life Guards Squadron, moved in the direction of the firing. The advanced guard squadron took up a position above Nery and it was joined soon after by the rest of the Brigade. The German machine-gun fire was heavy, but fortunately it was short and the Brigade escaped damage. Lieut. P. V. Heath, Royal Horse Guards, was now sent forward with his troop and seeing a dismounted party of the enemy he promptly charged them. The Germans retired at once and Lieut. Heath dismounted his men and opened fire. As the weakness of this diversion became apparent the Germans at once counter-attacked and drove back the small force. In getting away several horses were hit, five men wounded, and Lieut. Heath himself was mortally wounded.[1] The attack by this handful of men on the open flank showed, however, that reinforcements were now coming up fast and emphasised the danger to Garnier's flanks. The *4th Cavalry Division* was soon to receive a far heavier blow.

The volume of enemy fire all through the action had been directed chiefly on the more exposed portions of the 1st Cavalry Brigade, and it was noticed that very little rifle fire came from the direction of the sugar factory. But just before 8 a.m. the Germans were seen by an officer of the 11th Hussars to bring up two machine guns to the factory and from there to open fire on the Bays, who were thus partially enfiladed. It appeared for a moment that a dangerous turning movement was about to be initiated against this open flank. It was at this instant fortunately that "I" Battery opened fire, and as the shells burst among the German guns the machine-gun fire from the sugar factory ceased and it was never re-opened.

But further valuable assistance was now reaching Nery and its effect on the action must be related. On the previous night the 1/Middlesex Regiment (19th Infantry Brigade) had halted at St. Sauveur. At 7 a.m., on the 1st, the battalion passed through Verberie and took up a position on the plateau about a mile to the north-west of Nery. Whilst this was being done heavy firing was heard from the direction of Nery, and a very excited Cavalry Sergeant-Major rode up and told the acting Brigadier (Colonel B. E. Ward, 1/Middlesex Regt.) that the 1st Cavalry Brigade was being "scuppered" at Nery and that it required immediate assist-

---

[1] The account of this incident is taken from *The Story of the Household Cavalry* Vol. III, pp. 50, 51, by Sir George Arthur.

ance. The Brigadier at once ordered Major F. G. M. Rowley, commanding 1/Middlesex Regt., to march to the help of the cavalry. The Battalion was extended on the plateau when this order was issued. Major Rowley realised that it would take some time to collect all his companies and for the furthest one to reach Nery. He therefore ordered the nearest company ("D," Captain A. F. Skaife), and the machine-gun section, under Lieut. W. W. Jefferd, to march at once to Nery, which could be seen distinctly, whilst the Adjutant was ordered to collect the other three companies and to follow with them as rapidly as possible. Having issued these orders Major Rowley went on in advance, and on reaching the northern end of the village at about 8 a.m. he met Brig.-Genl. C. J. Briggs and one of his staff officers. After briefly explaining the situation, the Brigadier told Major Rowley that the Middlesex could co-operate most effectively by seizing the wood east of Nery. From this position it would be possible to enfilade the Germans and silence their fire. Captain Skaife with "D" Company and the machine guns arrived shortly after, and Major Rowley moved them to the eastern side of the village. The company deployed outside the southern end of the eastern face with the two machine guns on its right. The German gun fire was still heavy and chiefly concentrated on the southern end. Major Rowley rode through the village to see the situation for himself. As he issued from the end of the village he saw the shells bursting on and near what was left of "L" Battery, the guns of which had been silenced. On the other side of the road the horses of the Bays could be seen lying dead in rows. Major Rowley returned to his company and his men opened fire just as he arrived. The visibility was rapidly improving and it had become clear enough in the last few minutes to see about a mile. After two minutes rapid fire the German gunners were seen to leave their guns and Major Rowley at once ordered "D" Company to rush them.

"I" Battery had been firing for about twenty minutes, and as the German guns ceased fire Captain Burnyeat searched behind their position for their gun teams and wagon line. This fire luckily caused numerous casualties among the teams which were then just coming up. The Germans made gallant efforts to remove their guns. One man, apparently an officer, was seen walking calmly about directing the operation and with a total disregard of the heavy close-range fire that was sweeping the gun line. The German gunners tried to run the guns back by hand, but the volume of rifle and machine-gun fire made it impossible to manhandle them back under cover and the venture had to be abandoned. It was clearly too late to save all the guns, but by rare devotion the gunners managed to get away four of them, and the machine-gun battery was saved, before the cross-fire of the British machine guns, the searching fire of "I" Battery, and the approach of Major Rowley's men caused the attempt to be finally abandoned.

"D" Company had charged forward on Major Rowley's order. The men crossed the valley, climbed the sharp slope on the further side, passed through the fringe of trees near the crest, and then dashed across the open straight at the silenced and now abandoned guns. To cover this advance more effectively Lieut. Jefferd took the battalion machine guns down the shallow sunken road behind "L" battery field towards the sugar factory. But in changing position his horse was shot under him and he himself was wounded by the Germans who were still holding the factory. The guns did not get into action.

When "D" Company reached the two abandoned batteries twelve dead and two badly wounded Germans were found on the position. The eight guns were apparently all undamaged, and on examination two were found to be still loaded. It was chiefly Captain Burnyeat's well-directed fire that had prevented these prizes of war, the first captured by the B.E.F. during the campaign, from being removed by the enemy.

About ten minutes later, Major Rowley saw the retiring German limbers about a thousand yards away to the eastward, but on being fired at the teams at once quickened to a gallop and got away. A few minutes afterwards a party of the enemy was seen retiring across the open about two hundred yards off, coming from the direction of the factory. Fire was opened on them at once, and one officer and twenty-five men then came in and surrendered. To render the captured guns as unserviceable as possible the sights were removed and the elevating gears and buffers were damaged. Altogether Major Rowley and "D" Company remained with the German guns for about half an hour before the party withdrew to Nery. Meanwhile by 8.45 a.m. all firing had ceased and the fight was over.[1]

While Major Rowley was holding the captured German position and rounding up stray parties of the enemy, the rest of the 1/Middlesex Regiment reached the village and came into action. "A" Company moved to the south of the village behind "L"'s field, whilst "B" and half "C" Company crossed the ravine to the north of the village and pushed on towards le Plessis Chatelain. The remainder of "C" Company moved through the village and eventually reinforced "D" Company just before Major Rowley evacuated the German gun position.

Immediately the firing ceased General Briggs ordered the 11th Hussars to follow up the enemy with one squadron. It would have been obviously unwise, under the existing circumstances, to have launched the whole regiment in immediate pursuit. Colonel Pitman, therefore, ordered "C" Squadron to cross the valley and to pursue the enemy, but not to push on too far. On "C" Squadron advancing, it was observed that not only was le Plessis Chatelain still occupied but that German transport could also be seen close to the houses. Arrangements were at once made with the one and half companies of the 1/Middlesex, which were also moving on le Plessis Chatelain, for the infantry to take up a covering and rallying position, in case the Germans should be in force and succeed in driving the squadron back. The dispositions were then rapidly made. One troop was to attack from the south, another from the north-west, while the rest of the squadron delivered a frontal attack on the hamlet. Colonel Pitman arrived just as the attack was launched. As the squadron closed it was met by a burst of wild firing, but no casualties were sustained, and pressing on the cavalry captured the place and many prisoners. A German ambulance was found at le Plessis Chatelain. One medical officer and two orderlies were left to attend to the enemy wounded and the other medical officers and personnel were made prisoners and removed.[2] The German doctors who were brought back in a G.S. wagon, expostulated loudly, both at being taken prisoner and also

---

[1] G.S. Diary, Cavalry Division.

[2] A detailed account of C Squadron's work at Nery, including the list of the captures it made, is given in General Pitman's article on *Nery*, (Cavalry Journal, April, 1920).

at being deprived of their revolvers; but the protest, though worth making, was correctly disregarded.

No further pursuit could be undertaken, for the original orders were definite. On no account was the small pursuing force to push on too far, and, at the moment, the rest of the German cavalry was out of sight. Consequently the prisoners were handed over to the infantry and the squadron was ordered to rejoin the regiment. The cavalry then moved straight back to Nery, dropping one troop on the way to assist in the removal of the captured guns.

All the other reinforcements reached Nery too late to take any part in the action. By the time that the 2/Argyll & Sutherland Highlanders (19th Infantry Brigade) had reached the southern end of the village all firing had ceased, and the Royal Warwickshire and Royal Dublin Fusiliers (4th Division) reached the front too late to exert more than a purely moral pressure on the enemy. The 2/Argyll & Sutherland Highlanders, however, were fortunate enough to find on arrival a much appreciated prize ready to hand—the breakfast that had been prepared for the 5th Dragoon Guards—and the hungry Scots promptly did justice to it. One regiment of the 4th Cavalry Brigade had already moved and occupied Mt. Cornon, a dominating and wooded height lying about a mile and a half south of the sugar factory. But, so far as can be ascertained, no effort was made by this force to co-operate in the fight either directly or indirectly, although placed well outside the German left, and its shortage of ammunition would have made the *4th Cavalry Division* a peculiarly easy prey. Possibly the poor visibility engendered by the mist, which did not begin to clear until after 8 am., may have accounted largely for this inaction.

When fighting stopped, the C.R.A. of the Cavalry Division ordered "I" Battery to send six limbers to bring away "L"'s guns, he also ordered Captain Burnyeat and eight men to go over to the silenced German guns; and the C.R.A. of the 4th Division directed XXXVII (Howitzer) Brigade, R.F.A., to provide limbers to bring away any enemy guns that were worth moving. Captain Burnyeat reached the eight German guns after Major Rowley and his party had withdrawn, and he completed the work of rendering them as unserviceable as possible. He noticed that three guns had been turned round so as to reply to "I," whilst the other five still faced

"L," and he noted that the four guns that had been removed all belonged to the northern battery. The wagons had been left by their guns, also some teams of dead horses could be seen lying in their traces behind the position, a perfectly fitted up battery commander's cart stood abandoned near the guns, and in a beetfield behind the gun position some wounded Germans were noticed. On making a closer examination of the captured guns Captain Burnyeat reluctantly decided that only three of them were really worth removing, and they were then limbered up and driven off.[1] Captain Burnyeat and his party returned to "I" Battery.

Considering the small numbers engaged the casualties during the fighting had been fairly heavy, for the British lost 42 killed and 91 wounded, and approximately 380 horses, whilst the *4th Cavalry Division* suffered a loss of about 180, of whom 78 were taken prisoner. It also lost about 230 horses, and left 8 guns on the field.[2] Proofs of the violence of the fight remained in evidence for a long time in thirty-two smashed wagons, open, empty gun limbers, all the saddlery and harness of the killed and flying horses, rifles, revolvers, preserved rations, tobacco, and clothes all strewn about on the ground. For several days after the fight dead bodies were being discovered and buried by the country people, and they also buried over 300 horses.

The German gun fire had done very little damage to the village defences, the strong stone walls had suffered little and the houses were hardly knocked about at all. The walls had provided ample protection for the 11th Hussars who held the eastern face during the fight and the casualties suffered by this regiment at Nery were only 2 men wounded and 2 horses wounded. Having taken up their position just before the firing had opened the men were well concealed, and on that misty morning the Germans never got a clear view of them, and distributing their fire along the edge of the village it proved quite ineffective against men who were holding such strongly built stone walls.

The task of clearing the battlefield, collecting and interviewing prisoners, evacuating the wounded, and reforming units occupied

---
[1] These three guns were exhibited on the Horse Guards Parade, and naively labelled "Captured at Le Cateau."

[2] For a more detailed list of the casualties see Appendix 3.

a considerable time, and it was not until about noon that the general retirement southward was eventually resumed by the Cavalry and the III Corps. (For the positions reached at night see *Sketch 3*.)

At 5 p.m. Kluck reported to *Supreme Command* that Lanrezac had withdrawn through Soissons and that the *First Army* had so far not established touch with the French Fifth Army, Kluck also mentioned the fight at Nery, and stated that he intended to reach the line Verberie—la Ferté Milon on the 2nd. But by 8 p.m. he had changed his mind. A British I Corps order had been captured and Kluck realised that the whole of the B.E.F. was in front of the *First Army*. Accordingly he informed *Supreme Command* that the *First Army* would attack the British on the 2nd, and after overthrowing them would be "at your disposal." But the B.E.F., by then, had slipped away and Kluck turned eastwards once more in an endeavour to fasten on the supposed French flank.

PART III. THE ESCAPE AND THE RESULT.

WITHDRAWAL OF THE *4th Cavalry Division.*

Sketch 5.

It was nearing 9 a.m. when General von Garnier reluctantly came to the conclusion that the fight must be broken off at once, and he promptly issued orders for the troops to withdraw and assemble behind le Plessis Chatelain where the led horses were formed up. The squadrons carried out this movement by rushes halting occasionally to rally and reform, and suffering only an occasional casualty before reaching the rendezvous. Just to the south of the hamlet the dismounted men of the *18th Dragoons* and the *2/Guard Machine Gun Abteilung* took up another position so as to oppose any advance from the direction of Mount Cornon, which would have threatened the division whilst regaining its led horses. No serious attempt, however, was made to interfere with the retirement.

After it had remounted the Division moved off north-westward covered by the *17th Brigade* and the *Machine Gun Abteilung.* General von Garnier desired at first to regain the shelter of the forest where he hoped to be able to re-establish touch with *H.K.K.II.* But fate willed otherwise, and the adventures of the division were by no means over for the day. As the Automne was neared a report was received that the British were on the other side, and directly afterwards shots rang out from the edge of the wood. The crossings appeared to be strongly held and ammunition to force the passage was no longer available. The direct way of escape northwards was closed, and so the division swung away eastwards in an endeavour to locate and then to work round the British flank in this direction. But, almost immediately, another report was delivered, and it stated that the British were in force to the eastward at Crepy en Valois, so this plan was clearly hopeless.

The bold manœuvre was now the only one that offered a chance of success—to strike southward in the direction of the old objective, Rozieres, in the hope of regaining touch on arrival there with the other two divisions of *H.K.K.II.* Garnier promptly decided on this course. But unfortunate delays occurred in traversing this unreconnoitred country. Immediately to the east of Rocquemont the sharply cut ravine, at the head of which the village lies, deepens, and through the marshy bottom winds a small brook, and this stream where the division encountered it was only spanned by a footbridge. A long and dangerous halt was thus imposed on the column which had to mass on the northern bank whilst first of all the four guns, followed by the machine guns, were taken across, and afterwards the regiments passed over in single file. Fortunately for the division, the village itself helped to screen this lengthy manœuvre. It was only when the *18th Dragoons*, the last unit of all, was crossing that long-range fire was opened on the cavalry, but almost at once the deep valley swallowed the retiring horsemen and the firing died away. Directly a path had been cleared for the guns and machine guns through the tangle of trees and undergrowth on the southern bank of the stream the march was resumed and at a more rapid pace, for it was clear that the pursuit had not been entirely shaken off. In reality the *4th Cavalry Division* was in a most precarious position. To the east of it, and rapidly closing in, was the 5th Division, retiring from Crepy to Nanteuil, whilst to the westward was the III Corps, falling back towards Rozieres and Baron, and several incidents occurred as the narrow corridor of escape gradually lessened in width.

The 1/Bedfordshire Regiment (Lieut.-Colonel C. R. J. Griffith, D.S.O.) forming part of the 15th Infantry Brigade, 5th Division, had been in bivouac at Crepy on the morning of the 1st September. At 8 a.m. Major W. Allason's company was sent up to support the outpost line when it was attacked by the *Jäger* battalions of *H.K.K.II*. At the same time firing was also heard in the direction of Nery and it was supposed that the 4th Division must be engaged with the enemy. About 9 a.m. Major Allason was ordered to take his company and reconnoitre the road towards Rocquemont in case it might become necessary to move to the support of the 4th Division. About 10 a.m. Lieut.-Col. Griffith ordered Major Allason to move on to Rocquemont as the outpost line was coming back. The company then moved down into the ravine that runs towards Rocquemont, the very one that had previously delayed the march of the *4th Cavalry Division*. Rocquemont was reached about 11 a.m., and here some abandoned and looted British lorries were found with some killed and wounded Germans lying about. This convoy

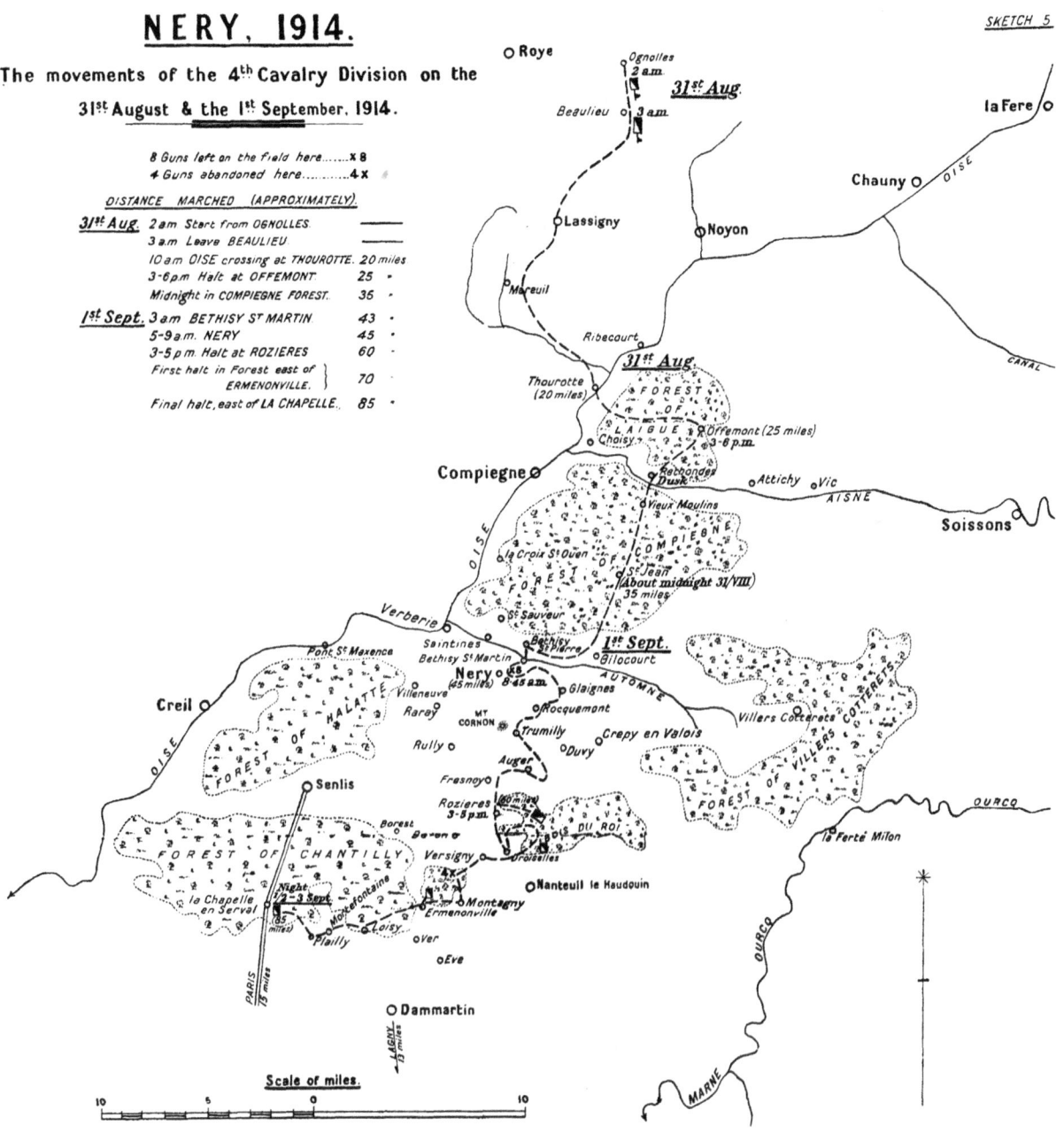

had been surprised by the advanced guard of *Garnier's Division* which had entered Rocquemont whilst the passage of the ravine was in progress. Major Allason rode some distance further to the westward but could see no signs of troops, and so about 1 p.m. he decided to move the company back to Duvy. Riding ahead to reconnoitre he met, at the outskirts of Duvy, Lieut. R.A. West of the North Irish Horse.[1] Riding into the village the two officers saw two mounted Germans in the street. As the Germans galloped past revolver shots were exchanged, and the enemy were then chased for about half a mile before they surrendered. The two prisoners turned out to be Lieut. von Wiedebach und Nostitz-Tänkendorf, adjutant of the *2nd Cuirassier Regiment*, and his orderly. The lieutenant's horse was hit and he himself was badly wounded in the thigh, and Lieut West's horse was also wounded. On searching the German officer Major Allason found a map showing the positions of all the advanced German units on the previous night,[2] and this was handed that afternoon to General Sir C. Fergusson, commanding the 5th Division. The German officer was too severely wounded to be brought away and he was left in a wayside cottage whilst his orderly was made a prisoner. On passing through Duvy a company of the 1/Cheshire Regiment (15th Infantry Brigade) was met. Some time previously this company had fired on part of the *4th Cavalry Division* as the latter was crossing the Rocquemont ravine. The Bedfordshire and Cheshire companies withdrew southwards together to rejoin the 5th Division.

After it had crossed the ravine, *Garnier's Division* moved through Trumilly heading southwards towards the wooded heights north-east of Rozieres. Occasionally a random rifle shot rang out but otherwise no incident occurred. On reaching the heights near Rozieres a halt was called, the men dismounted for a time, and the units which had become somewhat confused and intermingled were sorted out. Whilst this was going on a reconnoitring patrol, pushing on just beyond Fresnoy, exchanged rifle shots at a range of about half a mile, with the infantry escort to III Corps H.Q. The

---

[1] In August and September, 1914, A Squadron, North Irish Horse, was attached to G.H.Q., whilst C Squadron acted as Corps Cavalry in the II Corps.

[2] As the *4th Cavalry Division* had been entirely out of touch both with the *First Army* and with *H.K.K.II.* on the previous night, the dispositions shown on the map could only have been those which had been ordered for the 31st August. Very interesting information no doubt, but it was far from accurate as regards the actual dispositions.

encounter was short and sharp, and the mounted men soon fell back. After the regiments had mounted again they were drawn up in mass in regular order just to the north-west of Rozieres. The time must have been about 3 p.m. A long halt was now considered to be essential, for both men and horses had had great calls made upon their strength and physical energy and they had suffered considerably from lack of water and food, and from the heat of the sun. The halt, altogether, lasted about two hours, and during this time the large number of wounded were attended to. Oat sheaves were brought to the horses, but having been twelve hours without water they could not be induced to eat. This does not mean that they were incapable of any further effort, for, as the sequel shows, they responded willingly and gallantly enough to further heavy calls on their powers of endurance.[1]

After varied experiences the *4th Cavalry Division* had at long last reached its objective—Rozieres—but it was no longer in a condition to act effectively. Instead of being well placed behind the flank of a retiring and dispirited army it was itself encircled and hemmed in by hostile divisions. Naturally, on its arrival at Rozieres, it had hoped to meet its sister divisions, the *2nd* and the *9th*, or at least to receive some news of them, but these hopes were not fulfilled. As the hours of the long halt dragged on it must have become clear at last to General von Garnier that his division was isolated, and that he must now rely on himself and on himself alone to extricate it as rapidly as possible from the trap into which it had walked.

The III Corps report centre was already established at Beaulieu Farm, a mile away to the westward of the *4th Cavalry Division* when it formed up. This report centre was covered by a small detachment of infantry and machine guns belonging to the 4th Division, and this party was in position just to the east of the farm. As seen from the farm, across the absolutely open ground, the mounted mass of horsemen was halted in front of a large wood

---

[1] The war has again provided numerous examples of the courage and resolution of the horse. In November 1917, in the operations in Southern Palestine, on more than one occasion the horses of the Australian Light Horse Brigades went for more than fifty hours without water. The horses of one regiment had their saddles on for forty-eight hours and during this period it was impossible to water the animals. In September 1918, in the pursuit through Galilee, the 4th Cavalry Division covered 80 miles in thirty-four hours without off-saddling, but nevertheless the division took part in the capture of Damascus on the 1st October.

and appeared to cover an area of about two hundred yards square. For over two hours the cavalry remained in this position—a tempting and easy target if only guns could be brought to bear on it.

Towards 5 p.m., as the 4th Division was approaching the neighbourhood, Brig.-Genl. Phipps-Hornby, V℃. (B.G. R.A., III Corps), rode up to Lieut.-Colonel C. Battiscombe, commanding XXXVII Howitzer Brigade, and asked for an 18 pr. battery. The field guns, however, were marching behind the howitzers and it was not possible at the moment to pass an 18 pr. battery to the front. General Phipps-Hornby, therefore, took a 4·5 in. howitzer battery, and pointing out a green field ordered the howitzers into action to engage a German battery in that field. The hostile guns, however, could not be discerned. But a mass of cavalry was seen and Colonel Battiscombe was ordered to shell it. As he was very dubious about the nationality of the troops in question, he proceeded to act with extreme deliberation.[1] Time slipped by and the opportunity had gone before a round was fired. The mass of horsemen began retiring and soon was completely screened from observation in the wood and a real chance to avenge Nery had been missed.

It was about 5 p.m. when the main body of the *4th Cavalry Division* moved off. Some time before this the *18th Dragoons*, who had taken over the duties of advanced guard, had marched southward to Rozieres accompanied by the four guns. In this direction only did it now appear possible to avoid capture. On reaching Rozieres the dragoons started to water their horses, but the few wells were inadequate to meet their needs in the very short time that was available. Suddenly the order to mount was given and the advanced guard once more took the road.

THE DIVISION BREAKS UP.

Possibly on account of some misunderstanding liaison was not maintained between the advanced guard and the main body, and soon afterwards the main body itself broke up into at least two parties. Whilst the *18th Dragoons*, who were accompanied by the four guns, rode southwards from Rozieres towards Droiselles, part

---

[1] In justification for this excessive care it may be mentioned that on the previous day our own cavalry had been fairly heavily shelled by our own guns, and naturally Colonel Battiscombe desired to avoid an immediate repetition of this form of co-operation.

of the main body, including a large party of the *3rd Brigade*, entered the Bois du Roi, whilst another detachment consisting of part of the *Hussar Brigade* and the *Guard Machine Gun Abteilung* branched off into the wood to the east of Droiselles. Quite out of touch with one another, these parties remained all night in the Bois du Roi and neighbouring wood whilst British columns marched by on either side to Nanteuil (5th Division) and to Baron (4th Division) without discovering them. It was only the shortage of ammunition that prevented the cavalry from making a surprise attack on the marching columns. Situated as they were that night, encircled by strong hostile forces, the full seriousness of the position was appreciated and a strict order was issued that men were to speak only in an undertone. After this experience their relief may be imagined when, late on the morrow, the advanced guard of the *First Army* came up and released them. For them at any rate the adventure was over.[1]

The Southern Party.

We must now turn to the party that had broken away southward. Shortly after passing through the wood between Rozieres and Droiselles an order was received recalling this force to Rozieres. On the return journey the *17th Dragoons* and some elements of the *Hussar Brigade* under General Count Schimmelmann were encountered. This latter column was quite out of touch with the rest of the Division and the staff. The two columns joined together and moved into the woods to the east of Droiselles. Soon the track got worse and the impossibility of bringing the four guns any further was realised. During a short halt an officer of the divisional staff appeared. He carried an order which stated that General Count Schimmelmann was to march at once to Versigny, where he would either find the staff or a fresh order would await him. Schimmelmann's detachment at once pushed on to Versigny, but there only disappointment awaited the General. There was no trace of any of the divisional staff in the

---

[1] A message in the Cavalry Division G.S. War Diary says that an overnight patrol, which had failed to return before morning, had reported seeing a body of German cavalry early that morning (the 2nd), on the high ground about a mile to the south of Fresnoy. This force was undoubtedly one of the parties that had spent an uneasy night in the Bois du Roi. It was probably watching anxiously for the approach of the German columns.

village, nor was there any order awaiting him, nor could he ascertain anything about the route followed by the division. An officer who was eventually found in the village could only say he had quite lost touch with the staff. Patrols were at once sent out in all directions to re-establish liaison with the rest of the division, whilst Schimmelmann and his column awaited news at Versigny. Protection on all sides was arranged for, bivouac sites were allotted, and at last the tired horses were properly watered. It seemed that a halt at least of a few hours would be made. Suddenly the post on the north-western face of the village sent in a report that hostile columns (the 4th Division) were approaching Baron, less than two miles away, and that other hostile units were also to be seen towards Nanteuil (the 5th Division). Once more the situation had become critical and eventual escape seemed to be well-nigh impossible, for with little ammunition available any defence of Versigny was out of the question. Schimmelmann therefore ordered all the units to form up at once at the eastern outlet from the village leading towards Nanteuil. The Brigadier and his staff then proceeded to reconnoitre from the north-west corner of the village, the only point from which an extensive view was obtainable.

The two dragoon regiments and the four guns were the first to reach the rendezvous. Before the return of Schimmelmann and his staff and before the *Hussars* and the other details had arrived, the senior dragoon officer, Lieut.-Colonel Baron von der Heyden-Rynsch *(17th Dragoons)*, promptly ordered the march to be resumed, thinking that, under the circumstances, every moment gained was an advantage. The two Dragoon regiments and the artillery followed him, and thus Schimmelmann's command broke up. The dragoon column, on leaving Versigny, marched south-westward. Moving along a valley in the twilight the column managed to slip across the open unobserved, and then immediately plunged into the large wood which lies just to the east of the immense forest of Chantilly. Moving along a narrow woodland track men, horses, and guns were almost at once engulfed among the trees and dense undergrowth. The column then halted on the track, pushing patrols out to the edge of the wood. Heyden-Rynsch hoped that, hidden among the trees, his column might find shelter and security for the night, and that it could remain concealed there until the German advanced guards came up next day.

We must now return to the remainder of the party under Schimmelmann. Left behind at Versigny the General collected the rest of his column and a little later he left Versigny by the western side. Working unobserved down the valley this column managed to reach Ermenonville. Schimmelmann halted at Ermenonville, and there occurred another of the extraordinary incidents of this extraordinary day.

Schimmelmann captures a section of the 4th Divisional Ammunition Park.

The 4th Divisional Ammunition Park,[1] which had halted for the previous night at Ermenonville, heard rumours early in the morning that hostile cavalry patrols had been seen in the vicinity. An officer and 50 men were at once detailed to watch the approaches from the forest. No enemy was seen, but reports came in that a strong force of German cavalry was in the vicinity, and so about 2 p.m. the Commander of the Park decided to retire to Dammartin so as not to risk the large amount of ammunition in his lorries. On nearing Dammartin, however, definite orders were received to return at once to Ermenonville. The lorries were reversed and the return journey was at once undertaken. The commander of the Park and the section commander of No. 4 Section now led the column in a car, with the former driving, the section commander reading the map, and the chauffeur sitting in the back. The column branched off the main road running through Ver and approached Ermenonville along the side-road from Eve. Just as

---

[1] *See Sketch 1.*
In August, 1914, a divisional ammunition park consisted of headquarters and four sections, its strength was 7 officers and 464 other ranks, and amongst its vehicles were 87 3-ton lorries. No diary exists for this particular unit at this period, but its early moves have been traced as follows:—
The 4th Divisional Ammunition Park had sailed from Avonmouth on the 15th, disembarked at Rouen on the 18th, left Rouen on the 23rd, and reached Amiens that day. On the 24th it moved forward to Bohain, moved back to Lesdins on the 25th, remained there on the 26th, to resupply ammunition if necessary in connection with the Action of le Cateau, and was involved in the retreat from that position, when it actually was nearer to the enemy than its own D.A.C. It retired to Ham on the 27th, moved to Breuil on the 28th, then on to Attichy on the 29th, and halted at Villers Cotterets on the 30th On the 31st the Park moved back to Ermenonville and halted there that night. Only once throughout the operations had touch been established with the 4th Divisional Ammunition Column. The Park all the time had received orders direct from G.H.Q.

the car was entering Ermenonville at the south-eastern end, a large body of cavalry was seen blocking the village street. At first the horsemen were thought to be French cavalry, the car slowed down, and then suddenly a shot rang out from the back of the car as, realising their danger, the chauffeur opened fire. He then disappeared from the back, and the body of horsemen, galvanised into sudden action, galloped forward. To reverse directly to the rear was impossible, as the narrow second-class road was quite blocked by the lorries. As the cavalry charged down the street, firing revolvers and carbines and with lances couched, the drivers leaped from their lorries, but then rallying some distance down the road showed a firm front and an exchange of rifle shots took place. The officer driving the car saw a chance of escape and reversed to the left rear down the main street of the village, but unluckily the car then ran into another body of cavalry in the middle of the village. Completely surrounded by overwhelming numbers the two officers could only surrender. The officers had time to notice that most of the six regiments of the cavalry division were represented, hussars and cuirassiers,[1] and uhlans. They noticed too that the horses could and did gallop, and appeared to be in fairly good condition, but that men and horses were both short of food. For this reason the contents of the captured lorries were fortunately quite valueless to the cavalry. Nor, owing to the lack of ammunition and the dangerous situation in which Schimmelmann's Column was placed, could the pursuit of the escaped drivers be pushed home. It was indeed rapidly abandoned and the lorries were left on the road untouched.[2]

It was now more than ever necessary for the cavalry to find a secure retreat for the night as rapidly as possible. The wood to the north-east of the village appeared to offer the necessary cover and protection, and the horsemen began to file off rapidly through

---

[1] One German Officer made a special point that a General (Graf von Schimmelmann) and a Prince (Prince Henry of Reuss, a lieutenant in the *2nd Cuirassiers*) were present with this column.

[2] Cavalry Division G.S. War Diary states that, at 6 p.m. on the 1st, Headquarters heard that an ammunition column of the 4th Division (actually, as we have seen, the 4th Divisonal Ammunition Park) had been cut up near Ermenonville. A fine example that ill news travels apace.

Early on the 2nd September, when the British cavalry reached Ermenonville in the retreat, several abandoned lorries of the Ammunition Park of the 4th Division were found there undamaged. Drivers were obtained for the lorries and 4 or 5 were at once sent on to the III Corps.

the village towards this wood. Here the undergrowth was dense and no view into the wood was obtainable from the road. The car was ordered to accompany the column, but it soon stuck fast in a sandy track. The German officer then explained to the two British officers that a rapid and silent retreat was necessary so as to avoid being caught in a trap. In this situation the column could not be burdened with prisoners, and he would be compelled to shoot the two officers there and then, unless they gave their word of honour to remain where they were until morning when they would be free. There was, under the circumstances, no military reason against this offer being accepted, and the promise was given. The German officer said good-bye, and then rode off with his men down a forest track. But at the tail of the column there was a German major, who knew nothing of this arrangement, and he promptly re-arrested the two officers despite their explanation. The prisoners were then led into the gloomy depths of the wood. Here a large clearing was reached, in which by lantern-light a conference was being held. In the general obscurity the clearing seemed to be full of horsemen. Once more it appeared likely that the two officers would be summarily executed, but finally they were both tied up to trees for the night. To avoid any chance of their escaping with news of this place of concealment, sentries were mounted over them. The cavalry could afford to run no risk of being atacked in their hiding place, for, short of ammunition as they were, immediate surrender must have followed.

All night long the captives could hear the movements southward of men, horses, guns, and wagons. In fact the 4th Division moving in the early morning to Dammartin passed along the eastern edge of the wood, and the cavalry brigades from the north edge of Chantilly Forest passed through Ermenonville and by the western edge of the wood, and even (as will be seen later) entered its eastern side, but no suspicion was aroused of what was really hidden so near at hand. Even as late as noon on the 2nd, when, searching for food, a German patrol reconnoitred Ermenonville, British troops were still in the village, and they remained in occupation for some time longer. A report in the Cavalry Division G.S. war diary says that, at about 1.30 p.m. on the 2nd, Ermenonville and Montagny were held by a troop and a squadron of German cavalry. A party of British cavalry attempted to co-operate with the rearguard of the 19th Infantry Brigade to capture these two garrisons. But the Germans cleverly eluded the attack and slipped back into the wood to the north. Then, owing to the retirement having to be continued, it was considered impossible in the short time still available to search the large wood with its thick undergrowth, and the operation was abandoned. The British rearguard thus narrowly missed rounding up Schimmelmann and his column. But the trial was then over for, shortly after the British had withdrawn, touch was obtained with the German advanced guard, and the two captured British officers were sent back to Baron and handed over to a *Jäger* battalion that had just marched into the place. Schimmelmann's column joined up with General von Garnier's detachments from the Bois du Roi, and Heyden-Rynsch's dragoon column was the only one not accounted for. To it, therefore, we must now return.

THE FINAL WANDERING OF HEYDEN-RYNSCH'S COLUMN.

The hot day was closing in a cool, damp evening that threatened to turn into a really cold night when Heyden-Rynsch's dragoons and the four guns halted on the forest track inside the wood. Covering parties had been pushed out to the northern and eastern edges of the wood. Darkness was falling, but around the horizon the glow of the British bivouac fires was visible, stretching on a great arc from Nanteuil, through Baron, to Borest, thus giving the impression that the devoted column was already surrounded by overwhelming numbers. For the moment, however, the enemy apparently was quite unsuspicious, but the situation was decidedly critical and it was necessary to be prepared if events should turn out unfavourably. The colours and guns had to be disposed of. An easily recognisable spot was selected and here the Regimental Colours were hidden, and, so as to render the four guns useless in the event of capture, it was decided to remove and bury their breeches. A most untoward incident then occurred. Suddenly there was a blinding glare and a deafening crash. What had happened? Actually one of the guns, which had been loaded when the fight at Nery concluded, had been accidentally discharged. Hardly had the reverberations among the tree trunks died away when the full effect of this disaster was realised. The hiding place was no longer secure. Doubtless British patrols would at once search the forest seeking for the cause of the detonation. But the practically defenceless Brigade could not risk another encounter under such conditions, and reluctantly Colonel Heyden-Rynsch gave the order to advance. The colours were taken from their place of concealment, but it was decided not to attempt to take the guns any further, and the teams were used as riding-horses.[1]

Heyden-Rynsch realised that with exhausted horses no further advance could be made in complete darkness along the rough forest road; though had Heyden-Rynsch only continued along the track his column would have probably stumbled on Schimmelmann's bivouac and the concentration of the greater part of the hunted cavalry division would have been safely effected that night. As it was Heyden-Rynsch decided to seek safety by retiring further westward, and as a first precaution patrols were sent into Montagny. They soon returned and reported it to be clear of the enemy. The column then left the shelter of the wood. It was no longer possible to maintain any real order of march, the horses began to show signs of actual exhaustion, they were unable to maintain a fast trot, some even collapsed and lay on the road. Their riders would then attempt to keep up on foot until fatigue, too, overcame them, when they crawled into the shelter of the wood and lay down there.[2] The column moved on shrouded by the intense darkness. After passing Montagny and just before Ermenonville was reached some abandoned motor lorries were discovered,[3] but so far no other traces of the enemy were seen. Ermenonville was now entered. Was it occupied or not? No challenge rang out as the column

---

[1] Rumours that German Cavalry was even then moving in the Forest reached the 1st Cavalry Brigade at Borest during the early part of the night, and a timely start on the 2nd was made, so as to ensure withdrawing before any considerable enemy force got in rear of the cavalry brigades which had halted for the night on the northern edge of the Forest. During their move southwards on the 2nd, and whilst they were around Ermenonville, they discovered the four guns that Heyden-Rynsch's column had been obliged to abandon overnight. On the forest track also were scattered saddles, equipment, and clothing, overlooked in the darkness the night before. But no further search of the wood was made, and so Schimmelmann's column escaped detection although hidden on the western side of the same wood. It was impossible to bring the four guns away and they were left behind in the wood.

[2] Some of these dismounted stragglers in their attempts to rejoin were wandering about the country-side for two or three days, and it is even stated that a few succeeded in reaching the outer ring of the Paris defences where they were then rounded up.

[3] Clearly the derelict lorries of the 4th Divisional Ammunition Park.

approached, but all ranks expected a sudden shot and the way of escape to be barred. Scarcely daring to breathe the horsemen passed through the place. The village street seemed endless, but at last the houses disappeared, the paved road came to an end, the open country was reached, and the danger was over. Another wood, the main forest, now opened in front of the column and swallowed it up. Men lost all idea of time or distance. They rode on half asleep, but always haunted by the possibility of suddenly blundering on the enemy and harassed by the uncertainty of how long the horses would hold out.

After an interminable time a larger village was approached, first came the paved road, then scattered farms, then houses, and they were in the village itself. It was Plailly. No lights showed anywhere. Once more the strain of suspense was nearly unendurable. Suddenly a bright light flashed out, a window was flung up, and a hoarse English voice bellowed :—"Where are you going?" No answer was given and the column filed by as far from the light as possible. Once more came the question. Still no answer. Then the window was slammed down and darkness reigned again. No suspicion seems to have been aroused in the enquirer's mind about the nationality of the column.

The line of advance trended north-westward, and Colonel von der Heyden-Rynsch made a last effort to reach la Chapelle en Serval on the main Paris-Senlis road. But the east was graying now, and dawn was at hand. Cover must be sought at once, for it was far too hazardous to consider continuing the march any further in daylight. Fortunately at this moment the road traversed a well wooded park which stretched on either side of it, and this gave promise of a certain degree of shelter and protection. Heyden-Rynsch decided to use it. The high wire netting surrounding the park was quickly cut, men and horses promptly disappeared in single file among the bushes, all tracks were effaced, the fence was repaired, and no signs were left to betray that here, within fifteen miles of the forts of Paris, a column of four hundred German cavalry was concealed. Bits were removed, so that by their jingling they should not betray the presence of horses. Then the animals were watered at the ponds, and afterwards the weary men and horses lay down and slept, each man beside his horse with the bridle wound round his arm or leg. There was nothing to reveal the hiding place of the exhausted troops.

Whilst Heyden-Rynsch's column lay oblivious to all that was happening, the British cavalry, continuing the general retirement on the 2nd, had reached Ermenonville. Here, among other things, were discovered to the west of the town some debris and two German cavalry horses. A squadron was promptly pushed out to reconnoitre towards Mortefontaine. On its return it reported that some hours previously a large body of German cavalry had passed through Mortefontaine moving west. Abandoned cloaks, saddles, etc., marked the way the enemy had gone. Inhabitants also stated that the horses seemed very exhausted. But the squadron commander decided that under the circumstances the enemy had gained too long a start and that further pursuit was unlikely to be rewarded. He, therefore, returned and reported. Yet within three miles Heyden-Rynsch's column was even then sleeping the sleep of utter exhaustion and was quite unprotected. The Gods who live for ever were on its side this day.

It was high noon on the 2nd September before the sleepers gradually awakened. But even now no unnecessary movements were allowed, though occasionally a man left his place to get some water. As for the horses, they lay still and rested, their thirst was at last quenched and they sought to relieve their hunger by munching branches and scattered leaves. To cover the resting column some officers lay out in the shelter of the undergrowth near the Plailly road and watched the traffic. Motors, cyclists, patrols, and occasional small units, all of them French, passed along, but no sounds of firing were heard. Never before had the *18th Dragoons* spent such a strange anniversary of the surrender of Sedan.

As time went on the officers on look-out noticed that gradually the traffic on the road was growing heavier. Sounds of firing too could now be heard. To the northward a bombardment was in progress, and slowly the sound crept nearer. Then a German aeroplane was seen, but it was impossible to attract the attention of the observer, and before long the French drove it off with heavy shelling. Once more quiet reigned.

Some time later in the afternoon an officer worked through to the edge of the Senlis-Paris highway and gleaned really important information. A long and heavy column of French troops was moving southwards in the direction of Paris (it was the 56th Reserve Division retiring). Infantry, artillery, cavalry, and transport, were all hastening southward, without even making an attempt to preserve any form of march discipline. The impression left on the observer's mind was that of a broken army carrying out a hasty retreat. Did this impression of the retreat of only one column reach Kluck during the course of the next two days? and if so what effect did it have on his mind in confirming his too-easily formed belief that Maunoury's Army was a beaten rabble?

The officer then returned to the bivouac and his report was received with general satisfaction by all ranks. But night was coming on again and the fate of the column still hung in the balance. Suddenly, away in the direction of Plailly, a heavy outburst of musketry was heard. The column was still hemmed in all round by enemies. All ranks were alert and ready, carbines were loaded, and arrangements were made to make a last stand with the few remaining cartridges. But after a short time quiet reigned once more, gradually the traffic grew less and less, until at midnight the main road was clear.

When the 3rd September dawned no signs of the enemy could be seen. Patrols were pushed out. Cautiously they felt their way both to la Chapelle and also to Plailly, but no traces of French or of British troops could be found. Then at 8.30 a.m. Colonel von der Heyden-Rynsch sent out an officer's patrol to establish touch with the *First Army*. Some time later the patrol returned and reported that near Ermenonville it had encountered the advanced guards of the *II Corps*. The column then fell in at once and moved to Ermenonville. It reached the village that afternoon. Here at last oats were obtained for the horses and some supplies were issued to the men. Then at 6 p.m. orders were received for the column to move on to Nanteuil at once. To its delight the column found its transport awaiting it, and at last the troops were able to obtain a hot meal before bivouacking for the night, and the horses were off-saddled for the first time during the Nery operations. On the next day Heyden-Rynsch's column marched on to Droiselles and there rejoined the *4th Cavalry Division*. All its outlying detachments having rejoined, and having been rearmed with four new guns to replace the twelve which it had lost, the division was again regarded as a fighting force. Although the actual Nery operation may now be considered to be at an end, yet its after effect was destined to be far reaching and momentous.[1]

THE EXODUS FROM DAMMARTIN.

During the afternoon of the 1st September it was recognised at G.H.Q., at Dammartin, that the German armies were once more closing on the B.E.F., and also it was ascertained that some enemy cavalry had actually penetrated the British front. Consequently at 7 p.m. an order was issued that the retreat must be continued as soon as possible and that the troops were to get clear of their pursuers by a night march. In the same order it was also stated that G.H.Q. was moving at once to Lagny.

Many reasons have been given to explain this sudden move on the night of the 1st September. It is only necessary to give one account. An Army Service Corps officer, motoring on duty connected with refilling points, suddenly noticed a Uhlan officer (who had been thrown from his horse) hiding in a ditch near the road, and secured him. The Uhlan was brought in to G.H.Q. in the car, and this proof of the unexpected proximity of German cavalry occasioned something like a stampede. The dinner, which had just been served, was abandoned, and headed by a senior officer, now dead, carrying a glass of red wine in one hand and a plate of meat in the other, the staff packed itself into motor cars, whilst another senior officer, who had some reason to know the approximate whereabouts of the enemy with fair accuracy, stood on the steps of the chateau and asked in appropriate language what was the reason for such a flight when there was not a German within twenty miles.[2]

---

[1] On the 4th September the *4th Cavalry Division* and the *7th Jäger Battalion* were left behind with the *IV Reserve Corps*, acting as right flank guard to the *First Army*. In other words a tired and battle-worn cavalry division and a rather weak corps were left to guard this vital flank at the crisis of the campaign. Kluck must have considered Maunoury's army was a negligible quantity.

On joining Gronau's *IV Reserve Corps* on the 4th Garnier pushed out two squadrons from his division to cover both the Oise valley and the line from Creil to Senlis. Fortunately this attempt to clear up the situation beyond Kluck's open flank could gain no timely information of the menace that now threatened the *First Army*.

[2] Except for the scattered columns of the *4th Cavalry Division*, without guns and practically without ammunition, this statement was a fair summary of the situation (vide Sketch 3).

However that may be, it is at any rate certain that on the next day, (2nd September) when the 4th Division reached Dammartin about 9 a.m. all the outward signs of a hurried evacuation were very apparent. Outside the deserted chateau tin boxes were lying about, together with files of papers, a typewriter, and a broken-down car with the chauffeur busily engaged on repairs, whilst inside, on the table, was a practically untouched meal.

To return to the move to Lagny. As night was coming on the powerful headlights on the cars were turned on, and the column blazing with light, like a gigantic glow-worm, wound south along the narrow road to Lagny. Darkness fell, and the country-side was shrouded in an obscurity that was accentuated by the brilliantly illuminated road. Suddenly, on nearing Lagny, shots rang out in front. The long column halted and some consternation was shown. It was the ill-omened 1st September. Had the German cavalry already effected a complete encirclement, and was a German Cannae within sight? Finally, taking one of the headlights in his hand, the French interpreter advanced to reconnoitre. After a search he discovered a sentry post of some French territorials, *pères de famille*, ensconced in a ditch. Depressed by their cold vigil, they had fired on the unexpected and brilliantly lighted column merely to keep up their spirits, and fortunately had fired high. With peace restored, the column moved on to Lagny and reached the town about 10 p.m. Here, covered by the broad stream of the Marne, the plan for further operations was proceeded with. Others, as well as the *4th Cavalry Division*, will have cause to remember with mixed feelings Sedan Day, 1914.

SOME COMMENTS ON THE NERY OPERATION.

Most of the comments to be made on this action are mere glimpses of the obvious and we need not, therefore, weary ourselves by considering them. The adventure has been written in considerable detail because it is believed that it had an important bearing on the result of the future operations, and even on the fate of the Great War itself. Up till now Nery has often been lightly regarded as a mere chance encounter in a mist, followed by a spectacular fight. It was considered chiefly notable for the fact that one battery gained no fewer than three Victoria Crosses as a reward for the gallantry and devotion to duty shown by those who fought their guns to the end, in the face of overwhelming odds. But, apart from this aspect, it was said that there was no lesson to learn from Nery and that the action had no bearing on the main operations. Quite in accordance with this view is the fact that, by a singular oversight, no battle honour commemorates Nery, the action in which the first guns were captured from the Germans by the B.E.F., nor has even an Army List honour been granted for this fight, the result of which was to prove so eventful.

One of the lessons to be learned from Nery is the general consternation that is caused by hostile cavalry suddenly appearing behind what is believed to be the general outpost line. It has been pointed out earlier in the narrative (p. 322) that General Snow, commanding the 4th Division, was rendered most uneasy about the situation when he heard of the disappearance of the French troops from the Oise bridge on his open flank, and by the various reports which reached him during the night and early morning. But he, as well as everyone else, was surprised to find a large force of German cavalry with guns suddenly appearing several miles behind the line on which our infantry was supposed to be billeted. Similar examples exist in military history. Students will recall the consternation caused at *First Army Headquarters* near la Ferté Milon on the evening of the 8th September, 1914, by the sudden and unexpected appearance so far behind the German front on the Ourcq of the French 5th Cavalry Division (Cornulier-Luciniere), carrying out its famous raid. But a firm front was shown. Generaloberst von Kluck and all the members of the *Army Staff* "seized rifles, carbines and revolvers . . . . and extended out and lay down, forming a long firing line. The dusky red and clouded evening sky shed a weird light on this quaint little force." [1] The raiding cavalry swung northwards and thus narrowly missed making a great capture. Although the general situations were very different, one cannot help comparing Kluck's prompt defensive with the exodus from Dammartin only a week before.

Again it is interesting to speculate what would have been the result if the 1st Cavalry Brigade had moved off from Nery at the hour originally intended. In this case the *4th Cavalry Division*

---

[1] Kluck's, *March on Paris*, 1914, pp. 132, 133.

would have found Nery unoccupied, and no fight would have taken place there. But what would have been the effect on the retreat of the B.E.F. if a quite intact and fairly fresh *4th Cavalry Division* had been free to move about among the unsuspecting retiring columns? Undoubtedly a very complicated state of affairs would have arisen, great delay might have been caused at a critical moment of the retreat, and considerable loss would have been suffered before a sufficient mounted force could be collected to destroy the boldly handled division. The Fight at Nery saved the B.E.F. from facing such a difficult situation.

Further it is clear that in any chance encounter of this description, into which the element of mutual surprise is bound to enter, the opening advantage will always lie with that force which is on the move. In this case the 1st Cavalry Brigade was stationary and it was the *4th Cavalry Division* that was on the move. The initial advantage, as well as that of preponderating numbers and of a better position, all lay with the German cavalry. But General von Garnier did not possess indefinite time for his task; and a stout defence, combined with a masterly handling of machine guns and a prompt and bold counter-offensive, kept the fight alive and the enemy fully employed until reinforcements arrived and settled the fate of the day. In Nery as "in all dangerous operations one must act, not think."

This last maxim is also well illustrated by General von Garnier's handling of his division in the situation that faced him at 9 a.m. on the 1st September. Defeated at Nery, with the enemy behind him and on both flanks, and hostile reinforcements closing in on his division, he did not lose heart but acted promptly and took the boldest and most unexpected course. In this way he saved his division. But even so, in any analagous situation it is less difficult for a mounted force to escape capture by shrewd, determined leadership and a skilful use of available cover, than it is to concentrate and combine several independent columns and then round up the isolated force. The difficulties of the latter operation are accentuated a hundredfold when the pursuers are themselves part of a force retreating rapidly in front of a victorious enemy, and cannot remain on the ground for any length of time. In that case, as was shown in these operations, only concealment for a comparatively short time was necessary and the hunted force actually suffered little more than great fatigue, considerable discomfort, and some measure of alarm.

But the real importance of the Nery operation is far greater and its significance far deeper. As a result of its handling in the Fight at Nery, its weariness resulting from its adventures after the fight, and because it only possessed one battery of 4 guns, the *4th Cavalry Division* was relegated from the 4th September (inclusive) to perfunctory right flank-guard work in co-operation with the *IV Reserve Corps*. Considering the known state of this cavalry division, it is curious that General von Kluck did not attach any aircraft to his flank guard. But Kluck's eyes now gazed south and he did not vouchsafe even a glance towards Paris. As a result of its battle-worn condition *Garnier's Division* for the moment, the critical moment, was naturally no longer capable of effective far-flung reconnaissance on the open vital flank of the *First Army*, which was now hastening on to be in at the death between the Marne and Seine. Indeed the *4th Cavalry Division* was refused in the Oise valley behind the German right. As a result, early on the fatal 5th September, *Gronau's Corps* blundered across the front of Maunoury's reorganised army. In a flash the changed situation was recognised. An enemy was in position beyond the open flank— who was he? and in what strength? As neither a fighting force of cavalry, nor aeroplanes, were available, Gronau had to engage his infantry and guns in an attempt to clear up the situation. The corps became closely involved, the French hung on stubbornly, news filtered back slowly, and considerable time elapsed before the truth was ascertained. Actually it was not until about 10 p.m. that Kluck heard by telephone from one of his other corps commanders that *Gronau's Corps* had become involved with the enemy on the 5th. Then about two hours later came another telephone message giving rather fuller particulars. He now heard that Gronau had blundered onto an enemy who was in superior strength, that severe fighting had taken place, and that the *IV Reserve Corps* had been forced back. Then, at last, he realised something of the serious nature of the actual situation. But golden hours had been wasted on the 5th that could have been saved by early and bold reconnaissance, had only Gronau been properly equipped for his task. It was not therefore until the 6th that Kluck could issue orders to his other corps who were still racing south. Consequently they had pressed further forward and time had sped by before any reinforcements could reach Gronau, who was confronting an ever-growing force of enemies.

If Gronau had been supplied with aeroplanes, and if the *4th Cavalry Division* had still been a fresh and effective fighting formation and capable of bold reconnaissance work on the open right wing, Maunoury's Army in position would have been discovered on the early morning of the 5th September. Backed by a display of force by Gronau, sufficient information should have reached Kluck early enough that afternoon to enable him to issue orders to his other corps. This should have resulted in effective action being taken against Maunoury early on the 6th September, and before the *IV Reserve Corps* had become exhausted.

As it was a radical change came over the operations. The invading flood of the German hosts reached high watermark. Then came the turn of the tide. As a result of the advance of the B.E.F. into the ever-widening gap between the *First* and *Second Armies*, a hasty retreat was decided on; and as the invaders turned back sullenly from the Marne and streamed northward across the valley of the Aisne, it became clear that France, and with her the Allied Cause, was indeed saved.

Even if the German attack at Nancy, which was beaten back by the French, was the real Kaiser-Battle of this series of operations in September, 1914, yet even then a great victory was still not despaired of until the 9th September, when the fate of the Battle of the Marne was finally and irrevocably decided. With the loss of the Marne died all hope of an early success. So in this sense the Battle of the Marne may be regarded as the decisive battle of the war. For never again, in all the four long years of bitter fighting that were to come, were the German Armies to be so near an overwhelming success. The ruin of all their hopes at the Marne was largely due to the failure to locate in time the threat that menaced Kluck's open right on the 5th September as he rushed southward. This failure may be traced directly to the Fight at Nery.

APPENDIX 1.

ORDER OF BATTLE OF THAT PART OF THE GERMAN RIGHT WING WHICH WAS IN THE NEIGHBOURHOOD OF NERY ON THE 31ST AUGUST AND THE 1ST SEPTEMBER.

FIRST ARMY.—Generaloberst von Kluck.

II Corps (3rd and 4th Divisions)—General von Linsingen;
III Corps (5th and 6th Divisions)—General von Lochow;
IV Corps (7th and 8th Divisions)—General Sixt von Armin;
IX Corps (17th and 18th Divisions)—General von Quast;
IV Reserve Corps (17th Reserve and 22nd Reserve Divisions)—General von Gronau;
III Reserve Corps (5th Reserve and 6th Reserve Divisions)[1]—General von Beseler.

II Cavalry Corps (H.K.K.II.)—General von der Marwitz.
    2nd Cavalry Division—Major-General Baron von Krane;
    4th Cavalry Division[2]—Lieut.-General von Garnier;
    9th Cavalry Division—Major-General Count von Schmettow;[3]
together with the
    3rd, 4th, 7th, 9th, and 10th Jäger Battalions.

SECOND ARMY—Generaloberst von Bülow.

(Guard, VII, X, VII Reserve,[4] and X Reserve Corps.)

I Cavalry Corps (H.K.K.I.)—Lieut.-General Baron von Richthofen.
    Guard Cavalry Division—Lieut.-General von Storch;
    5th Cavalry Division—Major-General von Ilsemann;
together with the
    Guard Jäger, Guard Schützen, 11th, 12th, and 13th Jäger Battalions.

---

[1] The *III Reserve Corps* remained in Belgium masking Antwerp. It was reinforced for the siege of Antwerp by the *4th Ersatz Division* (from Lorraine). This division reached Brussels on the 25th September.

[2] A detailed order of battle of the *4th Cavalry Division* is given below in Appendix 2.

[3] Until the 12th August Major-General von Bülow was in command of the *9th Cavalry Division*.

[4] The *VII Reserve Corps* remained behind to carry out the siege of Maubeuge (25th August-7th September). The corps did not begin its southward march until the 10th September.

Previously to this the *Guard Reserve Corps*, (*Second Army*) and the *XI Corps* (*Third Army*) had been left to undertake the siege of Namur (21st-25th August). After this fortress fell these two corps were sent to the Eastern Front, and neither of them entered France in 1914.

APPENDIX 2.

Order of Battle, *4th Cavalry Division.*

General Officer Commanding—Lieut.-General O. von Garnier.[1]

3rd Cavalry Brigade—Colonel Count von der Goltz.

    2nd Cuirassiers (Kürassier-Regiment Königin, Nr. 2)—Lieut.-Colonel von Knobelsdorff;

    9th Uhlans (Pommersches Ulanen-Regiment, Nr. 9)—Lieut.-Colonel Count von Schmettow.

17th Cavalry Brigade—Major-General Count von Schimmelmann.

    17th Dragoons (Grossherzoglich Mecklenburgisches Dragoner-Regiment, Nr. 17)—Lieut.-Colonel Baron von der Heyden-Rynsch;

    18th Dragoons (Grossherzoglich Mecklenburgisches Dragoner-Regiment, Nr. 18)—Captain von Anderten (from the *17th Dragoons*).[2]

18th Cavalry Brigade—Colonel von Printz.

    15th Hussars (Husaren-Regiment Königin Wilhelmina der Niederlande, Nr. 15)—Major von Zieten;

    16th Hussars (Husaren-Regiment Kaiser Franz Joseph von Osterreich, König von Ungarn, Nr. 16)—Lieut.-Colonel Paul Ludendorff.

1st Horse Artillery Abteilung (3rd Field Artillery Regiment)[3] *(Feldartillerie-Regiment General-Feldzeugmeister (I Brandenburgisches), Nr. 3)*—Captain Winckler.[4]

---

[1] General Otto von Garnier was 56 years old in 1914, having been born in May 1859. He obtained his first commission in 1878, became Major-General in 1910, and Lieut.-General in 1913. In 1917 he was promoted *General der Kavallerie*, and he retired on the 21st March, 1918. From September 1916 until August 1917 General von Garnier commanded the *V Reserve Corps*, and from the latter date, until his retirement, the *VII Reserve Corps*.

[2] Captain von Anderten took over command of the *18th Dragoons* on the 17th August, as the previous commanding officer, Major Baron Digeon von Monteton, and his adjutant were both killed on the 12th August leading an attack during the Fight at Haelen.

[3] It was organised in 3 four-gun batteries. It is abbreviated R./FA.3. on sketch 4.

[4] The previous commanding officer, Major Wagner, was killed on the 26th August near Bethencourt during the Action of le Cateau.

2nd Guard Machine Gun Abteilung (Garde-Maschinengewehr-Abteilung, Nr. 2)[1]—Captain von Schierstädt.

Engineer Detachment.

Signalling Detachment (with No. 18 Heavy Wireless and No. 10 Light Wireless Stations).

Motor Transport Column.

NOTE.—In 1914 the War Establishment of a German Cavalry Division was approximately 5200 all ranks, 5600 horses, 12 horse-artillery guns, and 6 machine guns.

---

[1] It comprised 6 machine guns.

APPENDIX 3.

THE LOSSES AT NERY, 1ST SEPTEMBER, 1914.

A. GERMAN.[1]

	Killed.		Wounded.		Missing or Prisoners.		Totals.	Remarks.
	Officers.	O.R.	Officers.	O.R.	Officers.	O.R.		
Staff, 4th Cav. Div.	—	—	—	—	—	—	—	
Staff, 3rd Cav. Bde.	—	1	—	4	2*	24	32	*Includes 1 Medical Officer
2nd Cuirassiers	—	2	1	9	1	21	33	
9th Uhlans	—	—	—	—	—	—	—	
Staff, 17th Cav. Bde.	—	—	—	—	—	—	—	
17th Dragoons	1	7	2	6	—	10	26	(The losses for this Regiment are not available.)
18th Dragoons								
Staff, 18th Cav. Bde.	1	—	—	3	3*	18	22	*Includes 2 Medical Officers
15th Hussars	—	2	—	4	—	14	23	
16th Hussars	1	4	—	12	—	4	21	
1st Horse Artillery Abteilung	—	—	—	—	—	5	5	
2nd Guard M.-G. Abteilung								
Totals	3	16	3	38	6	96	162	

If it is assumed that the *17th Dragoons* had approximately the same losses as its sister regiment (i.e. 26) then the total casualties suffered at Nery by the *4th Cavalry Division* were 188 all ranks.

HORSES. No totals are given by the individual regiments, but in a divisional report on the Fight the casualties are given as 232 (148 killed, 6 wounded, and 78 missing).

GUNS. Of the 12 guns, 8 were left on the field, and the other 4 were abandoned later on in the wood north of Ermenonville.

[1]* The *Reichsarchiv*, Potsdam, has most courteously furnished me with the above detailed list of the casualties to the personnel and horses of the *4th Cavalry Division*, and I particularly wish to record my most grateful thanks to the *Reichsarchiv* for this invaluable and hitherto inaccessible information. The losses give the total casualties suffered on the 1st and 2nd September; but, under the known circumstances, it is fair to attribute them all to Nery.

B. BRITISH. The British Casualties were as follows:—

	Killed.		Wounded.		Horses.
	Officers.	O.R.	Officers.	O.R.	
1st Cavalry Bde. H.Q.	1	—	—	—	[150(approx.)]
Queen's Bays	1	8	8	31	60–80
5th Dragoon Guards	—	7	2	11	2
11th Hussars	—	—	—	2	
"L" Battery, R.H.A.	3	20	2	29	150
Royal Horse Guards. (4th Cav. Bde.)	1	—	—	5	7 (about).
1st Middlesex Regt. (19th Inf. Bde.)	—	—	1	—	1
Totals	7	35	13	78	370–390

www.ingramcontent.com/pod-product-compliance
Lightning Source LLC
Chambersburg PA
CBHW080449110426
42743CB00016B/3325